AFRICA'S IDENTITY REVOLUTION
IN THE 21ST CENTURY

DAINESS M. MAGANDA

Published by Freedom Life Books, an imprint of ELOHAI International Publishing & Media
P.O. Box 1883
Cypress, TX 77410
Website: www.freedomlifebooks.com

ISBN: 978-1-953535-56-6

Printed in the United States of America

TABLE OF CONTENTS

DEDICATION

To the people whose identity is questioned, misunderstood, misused, undermined, deconstructed, and devalued, your lives matter and the stories you tell are footprints that inspire us to discover what it means to be human. To the African men and women who search and yearn for humanity to recognize and honor your identity, your presence means more than you will know. We salute your knowledge and beauty; your journeys continue to paint wonderful colors in the rainbow of humanity. Know yourself, value yourself, and accept yourself.

ACKNOWLEDGMENTS

This book is a result of multiple topics that arose from class discussions: Culture and Identity Linkages of the Swahili with the Outside World II. I thank my students, who wrestled with many issues of identity and sought to understand and learn more about the intricate topic of identity struggles, especially for Africans. Your persistent questions propelled me to analyze, reconsider, and explore ways to present identity matters through the eyes of Africans in a way that allows others to examine their own perceptions of identity and that of people different from them. I thank Dr. Lioba Moshi for her personal experience, academic expertise, and contribution when we taught classes together. I thank Dr. Sabnam Gosh for her input and suggestions on academic resources and possible topics to examine. I thank Dr. Fabian Maganda for his scholarly advice and input on key resources and activities that students will find engaging and practical. I thank my children, Dennis and Enock, for their critical questions causing me to explain why I am proud to be African and why they need to know the value of their heritage. I cannot forget my family and friends who encouraged me throughout the process. I am especially grateful for the wisdom and openness of my students who shared their struggles and ideas on identity matters; you made me dare to welcome others to ponder and reflect on our varied identities.

SALUTATION

Africa My Africa

Will there be a day when the world will embrace
you with joy and cherish your beauty?

Will there be a day when the world will want to
speak your language because it matters to them?

Will there be a day when people will see
your tongues written everywhere?

Will there be a day when people will be proud of you?

Will there be a day when people will run to you for answers?

Will there be a day when POVERTY will not define you?

I wish somebody knew how much I love you,

I wish EVERYBODY knew how much I cherish you,

Africa my Africa, even if no one else does,

I will tell them of who you are.

My brothers and sisters of Africa, let us rise,

Let the world feel our tears,

Let the world feel our strength,

Let the world feel our pride,

Let the world see how we are in love with our African soul.

PREAMBLE

EACH OF US has histories we are proud of, but if we are honest, somewhere in our lives, we find areas we wish were not there. To foster an environment of honesty and openness, this book welcomes you to think deep within yourself and reflect on various aspects of your identity. I believe life brings so many adversities and blessings. Our perceptions of lives' joys depend on the hardships we have endured. As we reflect on our yesterdays and look at our todays, we are awarded the dreams likely to surface tomorrow. Our past journeys inspire the visions we have for tomorrow, as a result, what we are today is a summation of where, how, when, and why we are. We think and see the world through the paths we have taken. Many people wonder why we all dream, worry, marvel, and even question the occurrence of different circumstances in our lives. But many forget that the beauty of such wonderings is what births the intricate synthesis of this world while enabling us to hope for a better tomorrow.

Born in Africa, Sub-Saharan Africa, East Africa, in the beautiful country of Tanzania, I looked at the world rather differently from how I see it since I stepped foot in the United States of America. Some say I have struggled too much, but I say my journey has taken me to great places and continually allows me to cherish my past, reflect on it, and envision a new future of Africa and of the world. When I struggle to answer many questions, I call on the memories, the wonderings, the laughter, the questions, and the words that have carried me through each moment. I talk to my mind, to my friends, to my enemies, to my leaders, to my children, to my family, to my students, and even more, I talk to my heart.

To get you thinking about Africa's identity revolution, it is important to examine critical factors that define and shape perceptions of identity that expose why many Africans struggle to accept their identity. Not all Africans have negative attitudes about being African, but most of them do. For you to benefit from the contents of this book, I highlight information that forms the foundation of the topic at hand. I must add, some of what people believe about Africans is correct, but some are myths that most believe without knowing why or, even worse, many think they know but do not really understand reasons that cause so many, not just Africans, to wrestle with some aspects of their identity. To start, I ask you to begin by answering the following questions that will be considered in this book.

    a.   Does it matter how people think about you?

    b.   Do you know why language matters in shaping how people see themselves and how the world thinks about them?

    c.   Why do most Africans, especially the educated ones, have a negative attitude about being Africans? This question allows us to examine institutions that play a great role in putting Africans in two different camps: the Africans who cherish their traditional ways of life while others wish to discard everything marked with anything African.

    d.   Which African traditions are mostly despised, and how does that make those who love them feel?

    e.   Has Africa benefited, if at all, from Western education? If so, in what ways?

f.   Is there more than one type of identity, and do other Africans in the diaspora struggle with who they are? Why or why not?

g.   What elements of identity define many Africans? What role does poverty, education, skin, or name play in a person's identity? What does poverty look like in Uganda? Does the color of your skin define you?

h.   Have any Africans in the Diaspora and in Africa transcended general perceptions about Africans? If yes? Who and how did they do it?

This book will show several factors that contribute greatly to how Africans view themselves, considering the aftermath of colonialism and the education system put in place post-independence. The use of foreign languages during and after most African countries received their freedom made it possible for African languages to be undermined. The devaluing of other traditions, ways of life, indigenous education, and religion, to name just a few, watered the seeds of the inferiority complex that took root during colonization. The African mind was rendered captive until it redeemed itself by learning about its colonizer. Alas, if only it was one power that dominated Africa, perhaps that would help, unfortunately or fortunately, Africa had many to call its master. But the redemption began when some discovered avenues of freedom by claiming the value of what they were led to believe otherwise. Lest you look so sadly on the African men and women, remember subjugation did not just occur in Africa, other parts of the world experienced it too. Therefore, identity matters touch all of us; thus, the book will explore other identity elements such as beauty, name, skin color, and race—using Africans' experiences to examine such matters.

The book will show ways in which Africans can think positively about their identity by following the examples of others who have been able to do so. I draw from poet Okot p'Bitek's work (2013),

Song of Lawino and Song of Ocol that offer a critique of Africans who embrace European ideas while despising their traditional beliefs; p'Bitek addresses identity concerns that most Africans deal with. I also use various films to illustrate how struggles such as poverty are intertwined with issues of identity, just like skin color cannot be separated from a person's welfare. The discussion highlights the complexities of both modern and traditional ways of living for an African whose identity is tangled in both; it underlines the struggle between the need to maintain a sense of African identity while seeking to move with the world at large.

CHAPTER 1

WHY THIS BOOK?

THIS BOOK CONSIDERS how foreign forces have, over the years, played a critical role in shaping how Africans think about themselves and why. The discussions in this book recognize how personal and collective image is vital in many aspects of people's lives. Unlike other books on identity that focus on this topic from a scientific or psychological point of view, this book brings together various topics on identity while focusing on the intricate nature of Africans' identity by examining historical contexts that shape ways in which political and social forces molded the world's view of Africans. It examines important elements that resulted in a tainted image of Africans based on various political and historical circumstances such as colonization and an education system that undermined the value of Africans in the local, national, continental, and global economy.

Most books on this topic tend to focus on identity and African culture, self-identity as an African, and Africa's identity crisis, thus painting a broad brush to issues that need to be specifically scrutinized as small elements that contribute to a big picture. For example, foreign languages in Africa receive attention from language scholars, while economic researchers look at poverty in Africa as a key element to a poor perception of Africa by Africans and the world at large. Others delve into notions of time and Africans' lack of time management as a major contributor to their detrimental economy. This, in turn, results in perpetual poverty that, ultimately, causes their dependence on foreign countries, which fuels their thinking lowly about themselves. Some seek to show various elements of African culture, including meaning and manifestations of beauty, without showing the reality of a departure to such standards by many Africans today.

In this book, I try to merge the historical and political contexts that underscore the connectedness of various elements of identity that led to a divided Africa, the elite—the ones who look down on their African nature, and the mass that cherish it. I attempt to use examples of Africans such as a prominent poet, Okot p'Bitek, Africans in the diaspora such as former president Barak Obama, and the late Dr. Maya Angelou, while illustrating issues of identity struggles through real-life stories of Phiona Mutesi of Uganda and Sandra Lang of South Africa. The book is a great tool in the class; it provides questions that foster critical reading of historical accounts while paying attention to modern trends that cannot be ignored. I also highlight the work of the late president of Tanzania, Dr. John Pombe Magufuli, to underscore a possible progressive future of Africa's identity. The book is also a great asset for those who wish to examine their own sense of identity and want to reclaim areas of their lives they once despised based on other people's opinions. Students and other readers will also be shown, through this book, beliefs and viewpoints about the African people. The thoughts presented in this book will be a resource to teachers who focus on Africa, culture, and identity in the 21st century and add greatly to anyone wishing to know more about various facets of identity, especially from an African perspective.

Overview

This book is divided into three major sections: language, culture, and identity. In the first part, readers get a background on language in general, language attitude, language and literature, language ideology, and language development in Africa. Readers are given the opportunity to understand the critical role and place of language in any dialogue regarding Africa herself and the international community. Here, I explain that language is crucial in key aspects of life, including politics, and cannot be undermined; however, once devalued, a people's position suffers, more specifically, Africa's perception of itself suffers, leading to a detrimental perception of its languages and their potential to propel Africa positively in the future. Readers see why it is logical for many Africans to think lowly of their languages and why many want to disassociate themselves with this vital element of their identity. I also show positive trends showing Africa moving toward a new understanding of its languages while illustrating the emerging popularity of Swahili abroad to the point that in the US, it is among the fastest growing foreign languages in institutions of higher education. Part two is devoted to culture. I define culture, its manifestation, and how it is cultivated. I put major emphasis on education and its role in shaping how Africans think about themselves and the world. I also present the Sukuma, a major ethnic group in Tanzania to illustrate features of African culture. The last part is devoted to identity and its various elements. Here, the various levels of identity are discussed and a connection between culture and identity is made. I give readers a glimpse of the tangled nature of the topic at hand as I draw from Okot p'Bitek's *Song of Lawino* and *Song of Ocol*. The section commences with critical discussions on naming, skin color, as well as race and identity, using an exploration of select films. I further illustrate how Africans in the diaspora and in Africa revolutionized the world's perceptions of African identity: I present the former president Barack Obama and the late Dr. Maya Angelou, as well as the late president of South Africa, Nelson Mandela and the late president of Tanzania, Dr. John Pombe Magufuli. I also share a sampling of students' reflections after engaging in the topics explored in this book and give a sample activity, "identity interview," that can be done to illustrate how teachers may use ideas from this book to guide students to apply what they have learned in meaningful and practical ways.

To better understand the topic at hand, let us begin by exploring the concept of cultural relevance and legitimacy in the post-colonial African context. Such a foundation is critical to grasp the reasons that led to acceptable and unacceptable actions by Africans as citizens in their own land and why Africa's identity revolution cannot be separated from the institutions that started it all.

Background on Africa's Complex Identity

Culture is a complex issue but is the foundation of everyone's identity. To understand Africa's intricate identity, we need to analyze the role of formal education in creating culture in the post-colonial context and examine the undercurrents at play concerning defining legitimate culture. Here I discuss the question of lasting and changing boundaries between endogenous and exogenous culture, which agencies play a part in defining and assessing such boundaries, which can be either collectively or individually shaped by formal education. Some examples to substantiate and illustrate the postcolonial African experiences are presented based on specific points I make. I will not delve deeper into meaning, characteristics, and forms of culture. I give more attention to this matter in the second part of this book. However, here, I give a brief overview of the term and offer critical examples of how culture and new traditions are created while paying close attention to the mechanisms for the inclusion or exclusion of new features. The question at hand: Is it possible to sort out legitimate cultural elements from new ones, and who can do so with authority and power if the knowledge they use is European and far removed from judging what should be part of the African culture? Later, when expounding the main characteristics of culture, readers can see why and how Africa's cultural revolution is possible when we understand our agentive nature in sustaining or revolutionizing prominent perceptions on Africa's identity.

Creation of Culture and New Traditions

Culture is defined in so many ways. Generally, culture is a cumulation of shared meanings or beliefs among a group of people. Ethnographically, culture or civilization "is that complex whole which includes knowledge, belief, art, morals, law, custom and any other capabilities and habits acquired by man (sic) as a member of society" (Okita,1992, p.176). A culture strives for identity and tries to preserve its uniqueness and distinctiveness while acknowledging the presence of structures that tie them to other cultures in subtle ways (Colbert, 2010). Because culture is learned, schools are institutions that play a vital role in shaping individual and collective cultural identity. As such, when colonizers created policies that racially discriminated and ranked Africans, formal education was given to the mass with ideals that benefited the colonial powers; thus, the natives only learned certain things to a limited level. Lumumba (2016) explains how colonial powers created two separate African cultures through education:

> "The French system, for instance, invented "higher primary school" for the "natives," which limited formal education

to a few years of elementary school. The Belgians also designed a system of mass basic education in which only the priests-to-be were allowed to acquire secondary and post-secondary/seminary education. Consequently, despite their relatively low levels of education, these men were most exposed to Western/European values in comparison to the vast majority of their fellow countrymen and countrywomen" (p. 20).

In doing so, the mass, the uneducated, those who did not acquire formal education had a shared understanding of their African environment and culture, while the educated became a different kind of African through acculturation into the European culture. When an African attended school, the colonizers were creating a psychological fence as well as a physical one with policies such as those that prohibited the use of African languages in schools. Though educated, however, the African man became uneducated in his own Africanism while the uneducated became more knowledgeable and connected to a shared understanding of his Africa. While missing out on important aspects of African ways of life and an education that is truly African, the ceilings created also made it possible for the "elite" to still feel a sense of difference, a kind of arrogance. In fact, such superiority was cemented by the high social and political positions the elites received not only during colonial contexts but even after independence.

What then were the new elements introduced to African culture? What then were the new beliefs and standards added to what most Africans believed? What then was the mindset born out of an educated African man? The response is not so easy. One thing is certain, to be African became so hard to define because the ones who could articulate it in ways that the world would listen were the "elite" Africans whose understanding of their Africa was tainted by the education they so well acquired. In fact, most African leaders were only the ones who were well educated. Which elements then can be given the crown of being "authentic" or "legitimate," and which ones are to be questioned, and by who? Although these questions are not new, I believe their answers pertaining to identity shed a new light.

Mechanisms for Inclusion or Exclusion of Cultural Elements

Knowledge is power. Upon the receipt of the so-called "European" or "Western" education, one thing was certain, identification of elements of what constitutes to be called authentic African culture was conceived (Bishop, 2003). Since the African "elite" knew how to use the education system to explain what and how to define "African culture," the political positions gave them the platform, among others, to preach the gospel of purifying it. Such efforts were made by some African leaders whose senses were awakened through western education. The process was not so straightforward, to say the least. In quoting J. Spear, Muscarella (2008) points out that "the assumption that 'subjective' stylistic analysis is distinct from 'objective' scientific analysis is a false dichotomy – which several honest conservators/scientists recognize. The individuals involved in both forms of analyses are subject to fallibi-lity (sic), ignorance, and error – as well as personal considerations, which include fear, intimidation, and dishonesty" (p.9). Essentially, in the post-colonial era, identifying and guarding what ought to be authentic African culture by the "elite" could be done by first and foremost an admission from western-educated Africans that they will need to have "qualification, ability, validity and legitimacy in articulating what qualifies as authentic" (Lumumba, 2016, p. 20).

To admit that the educated African elites have a contaminated sense of African identity that needs to be cleaned was a critical step. The transformational processes that would give them the right to claim to be the right doctors to cure the "cultural-contamination" disease they acquired was another form of education—one that would rid them of the miseducation (Woodson, 1990) and re-school them to African culture (Nyerere, 1967b). To that end, a group of leaders such as Joseph Désiré Mobutu, François Tombalbaye and Etienne Eyadéma renounced their European first names. In the name of purging Africa from the Western contamination, they also ordered all imported names in capital cities and rivers to be dropped; Leopoldville, for instance, became Kinshasa, while Zaire was a name given to what was Belgian Congo and River Congo. The former president of Tanzania, Nyerere, took a different approach; rather than just changing names and renaming places as other leaders did, he suggested a re-education of the African elite. The humble position of Mwalimu (teacher) Julius Kambarage Nyerere draws from studies that show the longer one stays in a particular education system, the more likely he or she would absorb the values embedded in such system (Lumumba, 2016). Thus, the quest to re-invent Africa to return to its pre-colonial culture was to have an education system that would have African culture as the key to measuring progress in all aspects of post-colonial Africa. Ade Ajayi (1992) explains:

> Our basic approach is that in our search for meaningful
> change and development in Africa, we should go beyond
> earlier strategies adopted in the anti-colonial struggles
> based on the opposition of tradition and modernity,
> culture, and science. The exigencies of development
> demand that we seek to mobilize the resources of our
> traditional cultures not merely in search of an ideology to
> respond to colonial propaganda and to assert that we too
> are human – that we built empires and we can sing and
> dance. Rather, they demand that we search for innovation
> and creativity and how to generate knowledge, skills, ideas,

and attitudes necessary for our survival and to sustain our growth. In such a task, our culture – that is to say, our values, our perceptions of ourselves, our sense of identity and solidarity, our understanding of nature, our knowledge of plants and animals – must be the essential tool for initiating and managing change (p. 25).

The need to create a new education system that is true African was not a small fit. But who and how will Africa decide on the content suitable for such a task? Only education is a panacea for progress; thus, a true African education must be founded on African culture. As noted earlier, purifying a culture and re-defining African identity by identifying the features that qualify to be "authentic" African was not easy, and in fact, such quest still goes on to this day. Perhaps it is worth noting that what African leaders did during the post-colonial era may have been an imitation of another culture, or did they really seek to re-create a pure African culture? Is it possible to restore a culture from its original value considering culture is dynamic, and to what extent does one conclude the transformation has resulted in the original form?

The concept of cultural relevance and legitimacy in the post-colonial African context is foundational to understanding the actions of individuals and groups due to their encompassing nature in exposing what actions are acceptable. Indeed, post-colonial histories regarding cultural relevance in expressing the notion of cultural "authenticity" that led to regulations in how citizens ought to behave in their respective countries cannot be undermined (Assié-Lumumba, 2016). Positions that considered African societies from a deficit model, backward, static, and primitive are Eurocentric in nature, and that is why examining them establishes a strong understanding of the topics to be further explored. Before you despair, with this poem, I welcome you to hope.

Hope

Hope is looking toward the future without forgetting the past.

Hope is looking beyond what seems possible.

Hope is allowing yourself to doubt so you can believe.

Hope is finding a way when everyone around you shuts the door.

Hope is dreaming, believing, stepping, and acting.

African and European Cultures in Education – Revisiting a Colonial Heritage

With a positive outlook of what Africa could be, African leaders matched forward to envision and act upon their renewed sense of what they believed to be authentic African. However, a discourse on African culture necessitates a review of the colonial legacy that altered life and identity for many Africans. To do so, a look at education before colonial rule needs to be examined. First, education was not systematic; for Africans, knowledge was acquired and transmitted through oral tradition, except for a few societies with writing systems (Bekerie, 1997). For most African societies, however, there was no reading or writing. Furthermore, before the introduction of European education, the younger received education from older members of the society based on gender. By doing so, cultural values, social institutions, and means of communication, to name a few, were passed from generation to generation. Marah (2006) explains:

> The process of traditional education in Africa was
> intimately integrated with the social, cultural, artistic,
> religious, and recreational life of the ethnic group. That is,
> 'schooling' and 'education,' or the learning of skills, social
> and cultural values, and norms, were not separated from

other spheres of life. As in any other society, the education
of the African child started at birth and continued into
adulthood (p.6).

Such traditional African education prepared Africans for life
using cultural devices such as initiation rites and rituals that cultivated a communal spirit among the youth while africanizing
its people. Furthermore, the griots of West Africa, for example,
memorized the history of their people and taught them publicly or
privately (Lumumba, 2016). As a result, there was a guarantee that
moral expectations and traditional values would continue for generations. According to Woolman (2001), African traditional education
involved training in all aspects of life, including intellectual, physical,
skills, and character-building, to ensure life within families and society at large is sustained. Later, however, a departure from this form
of education was introduced in the name of modernity. For propo-
nents of the former indigenous African education, Woolman (2001)
argues, a departure from it caused a desire to restore it, thus wanting
to reclaim and return to authentic African traditions, including a
call to use African languages in the education system. At the heart
of such an effort was a deep appreciation of education as an agency
capable of transmitting and causing changes that can be reflected and
altered when new environments occur.

Just as Africans used their indigenous education to Africanize
their people, so did colonizers use education to Westernize or
Europeanize Africans. Such education changed Africa's identity completely. The new Africa had a new mentality and values that defined
the educated elite. The question is how did that happen? How did
Africa go from having a thriving indigenous education system before
colonization to using the colonizer's education even after receiving
independence? Why are some elite—Africans still honoring Western
education while others wish to continue the purification process

put forth by the "authenticity/purity" leaders presented above? Such questions are not easy because the answers are multifaceted. One aspect critical to this answer is language. Thus, chapter two is devoted to key concepts on language and governance.

Discussion Questions

1. How do you define hope?

   _____

   _____

2. In your own opinion, who is qualified to identify features that should be considered the purest form within a specific culture?

   _____

   _____

3. If anyone is educated using a different education system when his own, does he or she have the right to show those who have not been educated in a different system that he knows more about his culture than they do?

   _____

   _____

4. Can you identify at least three people in your own family, hometown, village, or even school that you believe know more about your culture? If so, do you talk about what aspects of your culture that you appreciate and some that you're not fond of?

   _____

   _____

5. Among the people you know, your friends, your colleagues,
    peers, and family, do any of them still value their identity?
    Whichever identity you think is theirs.

    _____

    _____

PART I

LANGUAGE

CHAPTER 2

KEY CONCEPTS ON LANGUAGE

IN THIS CHAPTER, I present the intricate relationship between language and identity. Bearing in mind that language reflects individual beliefs and practices also shared in a community, here, you will learn the deep meaning of language and the need to understand the rules that govern a specific language system because anyone needing to learn a language in a specific community must learn key signs to communicate efficiently. The chapter will introduce the concept of language ideology, language and governance, and the complex nature of language and authority in post-colonial Africa. But first, a poem below expresses my wish on language:

I Wish

I wish languages were like water
I wish words were neutral everywhere

I wish voices were equal anywhere
I wish minds could know many things
I wish eyes could see everything
I wish hearts could love everyone
I wish the world could value every language
Languages have become a poison
They quiet the human voice
They ruin the human mind
They blind the human eyes
They corrupt the human heart
They dehumanize people
They let them hide the deep dark intentions of their hearts
They put a price tag on the voice of the human soul
I wish language meant people
I wish language meant the world
I wish every language was a treasure for the world
I wish language SHOWS all colors of humanity

Language Meaning and Characteristics

Language is the most powerful and major way of communication; it is multifaceted and can be defined in so many ways. Language makes it possible to express thoughts, desires, feelings, and I believe it is the best way to express emotions (Bickerton, 2009). Even more, through words, signs, symbols, whether spoken or written, such communication can be among two individuals as well as cultures or countries. Language is dynamic, always changing based on human experiences (Chomsky, 1972). Though language scholars have varied ways to describe it, the following five major characteristics differentiate human language from that of animals: language is arbitrary, social, symbolic, systematic, vocal, non-instinctive, conventional, productive, and creative (Scott-Phillips, 2014).

Language is arbitrary, meaning there is no reason a chair is called a chair and not a car, no relationship exists between the choice of words and the idea or object attached to it, once chosen; however, it stays as such (Hauser, Chomsky & Fitch, 2002). The arbitrary nature of language is the main reason we have different languages; otherwise, there would be only one language. Language is social. It is made up of meaningful signals that allow a specific social group to communicate by following a set of rules understood by members of that group (Berwick, Chomsky & Bolhuis, 2013). Thus, language allows relationship, interaction, and cooperation to take place. Language, in this case, is a social institution that provides establishment to relationships while allowing cultural development and nourishment to thrive (Botha, 2003). Language is symbolic. It is made up of graphological and sound symbols that denote meaning based on conventionally accepted meaning (Botha, 2006a). In other words, the logic of a language hinges on an accurate understanding of the symbols within a specific society. Language is systematic; there is a clear arrangement of symbols for them to make sense (Fitch, 2017). Each language has its own arrangement, which must be understood and employed for communication to take place; thus, a system that works for one language cannot be applied to make similar meaning using another language's system.

Furthermore, language is vocal; it is comprised of vocal sounds (Favareau, 2008). Writing is a representation of language sounds. Language is non-instinctive; it is conventional. No group of people sat down to create a language; rather, language evolves automatically through usage, making it possible for generations to pass it on to the next generation (Fitch, Huber & Bugnyar, 2010). For this reason, languages grow, die, and change. Language is acquired; it is not innate; thus, it must be learned (Ullrich, Mittelbach & Liebal, 2019). Language is productive and creative. It is possible to manipulate, modify, and arrange various elements of human language to produce new words or sounds, which can be understood between two people even if neither of them heard such arrangements before (Hurford, 2014). This is only possible because language morphs based on the needs of its society. In addition to the above characteristics, language can move across time and space and is culturally transmitted. With this in mind, we can all say that language is special. Every language is unique and has value, thus worth preserving (Ullrich, Mittelbach, & Liebal, 2019). Considering our focus on Africa, it is worth noting that Africa is credited with having one-third of all languages in the world. Such wealth is to be celebrated. Humphrey Tonkin (2003, p. 6) observes:

> "The diversity of language is an asset: it helps build cohesion in small communities and sustains unique cultures, thereby bestowing distinctive identities on individuals and reducing alienation and homogenization. The rich variety of linguistic idioms carries with it an equally rich variety of cultural forms and ways of thought and maintains for humankind a diversity of devices for coping with the uncertain challenges of human existence. And who knows what cultural and intellectual tools we will need in tomorrow's world? In this sense, linguistic diversity resembles biodiversity."

After establishing the meaning and key features of language, we can understand why language issues within any society shape and disclose what lies within people's minds and what transpires in their societies. Thus, we now delve into matters that cause people to rank languages, thus creating language stratifications, and for Africans, for example, factors that caused them to see their languages from a deficit model. To this end, let us examine language ideologies.

Language Ideologies

Language ideologies are belief systems related to and informing linguistic behavior as well as the framework that shapes decisions about language acquisition and use (Kroskrity, 2004). These can also be referred to as linguistic ideologies or ideologies of language. They are embedded with the structure, use, and nature of language while reflecting moral and political perspectives in a social world (Irvine, 1989). Jillian Cavanaugh (2020) notes that "language ideologies are this collective order, that is, the beliefs and attitudes that shape speakers' relationships to their own and others' languages, mediating between the social practice of language and the socioeconomic and political structures within which it occurs (p. 52). Language ideologies help us examine how minority languages are treated based on power relations discernable through language use. As such, they allow us to recognize ways in which language and various forms of inequality are connected. Scholars who explore power relations examined various factors that shape interactions. From 1970 to 1980, however it became clear that to some degree, power shapes all interactions; therefore, the relationship between language in use and power cannot be undermined (Irvine, 1989).

All societies under the sun have language ideologies. Community members, both official and ordinary, enact language ideologies, as well as academic scholars, official institutions, and the so-called elites. Kathryn Woolard (2021) elaborates: "Linguistic variability is socially patterned and related to the distribution of power and resources at both interpersonal and institutional scales. As the British sociologist of language Basil Bernstein famously put it, "Between language and speech, there is social structure" (p.1). As such, the power of language ideologies lies in their ability to shape and sustain social and political status within local and global societies. Woolard (2021, p. 1) continues,

"Ideologies are morally and politically loaded because implicitly or explicitly they represent not only how language is, but how it ought to be. They endow some linguistic features or varieties with greater value than others, for some circumstances and some speakers. Language ideology can turn some participants' practices into symbolic capital that brings social and economic rewards and underpins social domination by securing what Bourdieu called the misrecognition of the fundamental arbitrariness of its value."

Therefore, at personal and institutional levels, the distribution of resources and power fuels and shapes language variations. At the center of language ideology is the question of who determines communicative forms within a society. Is it the individual or the communicative behaviors already in place within a specific community? And do such practices play a role, if at all, in determining social systems? Language ideologies propel people to use a specific form of language in a particular setting for their own reasons (Cavanaugh, 2020).

Language ideologies manifest themselves in various places such as institutions, whereby shaping experiences of community members in ways that allow them to rank languages for special use, for example, choosing languages to be used for school instruction, formal writing, or media (Kroskrity, 2010). Due to its ability to rank languages and form symbolic capital, language, therefore, is a major force contributing to creating social domination (Yule, 2006). For this reason, language ideologies, by using ideas such as intelligence, authenticity, or personhood, play a great role in connecting various social features such as national or ethnic identities (Woolard & Schieffelin, 1994). As such, when languages are categorized into dialects, for example, a specific standard is employed that leads to deciding what linguistic variety ought to define a nation or an ethnic group. By doing so, power relations are created. This process gets complicated because "assumptions about the character of specific speakers or communities underpin evaluations of specific linguistic forms as, e.g., simple or complex, logical or illogical, rough, authentic, refined, or precise (Woolard, 2021, p.3).

Consequently, scholars on language ideologies such as Kathryn Woolard, Roman Jakobson, Susan Gal, Antonio Gramsci, Judith Irvine, and Jane Hill, to name a few, examine hierarchy and social inequalities in postcolonial contexts, troubling situations in which minority languages were put to compete against standard or national languages, thus exposing the interplay between power and social relationships (Schieffelin, Woolard & Kroskrity, 1998; Meek, 2007). I therefore use the term "LANGUAGE" as an acronym to highlight layers embedded in language and the ideologies reflected within its use. Language is:

Linguistic skill or expression
A communication tool
Nuance of identity
Gauge of global influence
Undisputable social and political sorting machine
Authoritative force of control
Great power that shapes and reflects the human mind.
Ever changing phenomena that defines human reality.

Language defines, reflects, expresses, and discloses people's lives while ranking them within local and global contexts (Hill, 2009). Language is not a mere communication tool; language embodies history, beholds the present while predicting, propelling, and controlling the future (Irvine & Gal, 2000; Gondo, 2010). With the help of scholars on language ideologies, we can examine the position of African languages after colonial rule and briefly consider possibilities.

Language and Governance in Africa

In postcolonial studies, language must be explored mainly because foreign languages of the colonizers were imposed on the colonized (Ndhlovu, 2008). Based on the notion that in multilingual societies, every language must be given an equal opportunity because it has the right to exist and flourish in all aspects of its society (Mazrui & Mazrui, 1998), African languages were not given the "right of language" nor "right to language." The former means, colonizers put in place language policies that deliberately sought to suppress African languages. As Mazrui and Mazrui (1998, p. 115) explain, the right to language is "the right to use the language one is most proficient in, as well as the right of access to the languages of empowerment and socio-economic advancement." Intrinsically, African indigenous languages were forbidden in critical areas, particularly in schools (Swilla, 2009). The few Africans who were educated during the colonial era

Punishment for speaking Luganda at school.
Image from Facebook via ThisisAfrica.me.

became versed in foreign languages in ways that planted a negative perspective about their languages; many of them re-count the humiliations, punishments, and even beatings they received if caught using their native languages, a practice that continues in many African countries to date (Ndhlovu, 2008).

Speaking a foreign language, such as English, for example, became a symbol of high social status because, in addition to other reasons, only sons of chiefs and a few in high positions in their communities could attend school to help colonial administrations (Maganda, 2017). Consequently, a formation of the African elite was created whereby only a few spoke the language of their masters while the mass was left unable to interact with them. Though they are children of Africa, upon re-education through colonial languages, such elites who tasted the sweetness of their indigenous languages were without a doubt given "formula," which was induced with all kinds of political and economic rewards, and without knowing, they found themselves rejecting their indigenous languages just like some children who refuse their mother's breast milk after experiencing the easy flow of the formula offered in a bottle (Maganda, 2016).

After receiving independence, some African leaders such as mwalimu Julius Kambarage Nyerere of Tanzania made efforts to re-educate and encourage his fellow Tanzanians to reject the colonial mentality, "kasumba ya ukoloni," by calling on them to reject using English and embrace their African languages, such as Swahili (Maganda, 2014b). His efforts were among a rare language-success story in Africa; Tanzania became one of the first countries to reach a near 78 percent literacy rate while also forming a national identity that made its fellow countrymen be proud of their African identity. In Tanzania, Swahili became one of the languages of instruction in primary schools and as a subject in secondary schools. Though helpful, indigenous Tanzanian languages were still not given any position in the education arena. Swahili became one of the official languages in conjunction with English, but it was not allowed in the tertiary level of education, thus allowing the master's language of English to still retain its position of power in Tanzania. Consequently, there was a mushrooming of English-medium schools in Tanzania that claimed to offer better education because children were able to speak English very well as opposed to their fellow Tanzanians attending public schools (Maganda, 2014a). Despite many studies showing students studying in Swahili doing just as well or even better when examined in their knowledge of subject-content areas (Brock-Utne, 2007), a language ideology of English supremacy was engrained in the mass; they believed, and no one would dispute that students who were able to complete their studies and spoke English well-secured better-paying jobs than those whose English were under par (Rubagumya, 2003). Such a phenomenon happened in other parts of Africa, such as Kenya and Uganda. The continual suppression of African languages was so detrimental to Africa in many aspects and started a downward spiral that contributed to Africans having negative perceptions of their own culture and identity. Zeleza (2006) notes:

> "All the languages of Africa invoke ontological and
> epistemological arguments, duly buttressed with the
> rhetoric and rage of cultural nationalism, that language is
> the carrier of a people's culture, it embodies their system of
> ethics and aesthetics, and it is a medium for producing and
> consuming knowledge, a granary of their memories and
> imaginations" (p. 20).

Consequently, when suppressed, the love and pride attached to African languages were erased. In response to such language discrimination, some prominent postcolonial African writers such as Ngugi wa Thiong'o, a Gikuyu writer from Kenya, advocated for the use of indigenous languages while others wanted to use the master's tool to enhance inter-continental interactions while also providing a progressive counter to a colonial history by envisioning new forms of language use to re-create a positive Africa (Ndlohvu, 2008). In Decolonising the Mind, Thiong'o (1986) writes in "farewell to English," language allows people to understand who they are and their place in their world. He likened the use of English in Africa as a "cultural bomb" working to erase a pre-colonial cultural and historical memory while instilling new forms of domination. His efforts to write in Gikuyu was a way of preserving it within its community because language and culture cannot be separated. He notes:

> [A] specific culture is not transmitted through language in its universality, but in its particularity as the language of a specific community with a specific history . . . Language as communication and as culture are then products of each other . . . Language carries culture, and culture carries, particularly through orature and literature, the entire body of values by which we perceive ourselves and our place in the world . . . Language is thus inseparable from ourselves as a community of human beings with a specific form and character, a specific history, a specific relationship to the world (Thiong'o, 1986, p. 15-16).

Thiong'o's perspective led one of my friends to tell many of us, his fellow Africans who look down on our own languages, to have a mental revolution. He said, "When a French national cannot speak English, Africans respect him. When a Spanish man can't speak English, Africans respect him. When a Chinese man cannot speak English, Africans respect him. When a Russian man cannot speak English, Africans respect him. When a Portuguese man can't speak English, Africans respect him. But when an African man can't speak English, Africans consider him a joke, illiterate, dumb, and stupid. We use

English as a yardstick to measure the intelligence of our people, including children. In our schools, children are made to believe they are stupid just because they cannot speak a language alien to their ancestral route. Africans referred to their language as vernacular— what a shame. Dear Africans, put an end to this mental slavery. Teach your children their mother tongue and allow the locals to feel free in speaking their native language without any stigma. Do not help the oppressors to extend their oppression." Likewise, when I think of African languages, I think of how I felt about my own language. I also think of how I feel now about my Sukuma language, my mother tongue and national language, Swahili.

The Language I Speak: My Shame and Freedom

When I speak, you hear the weeping of yesterday
When I speak, you hear the tongue of my tormentor
When I speak, you hear the voices of failure
When I speak, you hear the pathways of bondage
When I speak, you hear drops of my broken heart
When I speak, you hear rumbling winds of poverty
I have decided to speak with my own voice
This time when I speak, you will hear soft traces of life
And this time when I speak,
You will hear hope
You will hear strength
This time when I speak,
You will hear me living
You will hear me ruling,
You will hear me laughing
This time when I speak, you will hear prosperity
The language I speak WAS my shame yesterday
The language I speak is NOW my freedom
And let me tell you,

The language YOU AND I speak DEFINE humanity
Let me speak with NO shame
Let me Speak my Language of FREEDOM

With a different perspective, other language activists see the use of colonial languages such as English as an act of resistance, allowing them to remake a colonial language in ways that confront independent colonies in such that the use of English becomes a form of conquest, thus attaining freedom by using the master's tool. Salman Rushdie (1992) explains:

"Those of us who do use English do so despite our ambiguity toward it, or perhaps because of that, perhaps because we can find in that linguistic struggle a reflection of other struggles taking place in the real world, struggles between the cultures within ourselves and the influences at work upon our societies. To conquer English may be to complete the process of making ourselves free" (p.17).

The use of a language in ways that afford local adaptation to be reflected is a process whereby "the language is made to "bear the burden" of one's own cultural experience . . . Language is adopted as a tool and utilized to express widely differing cultural experiences, (Rushdie, 1992, p. 38-39). African writers such as Chimamanda Adichie do just that; she uses English to re-create Africa using English in ways that allow Africans in Africa and in the diaspora to tell their authentic African stories regardless of their various backgrounds. With such understanding, though abused and battered during colonial rule, a renewed sense of pride for the many African tongues can be born through a progressive path toward elevating their languages.

I am aware of the two camps on this matter; those who believe the only way to free African languages and give them the wings to fly is by Africans using them exclusively, while others believe the way to elevate our African languages is by using foreign languages to tell our stories for the world to hear. I believe both approaches can be used to various degrees to re-imagine a positive outlook on African languages. African leaders, I am convinced, have a big role to play on this quest. As stated earlier, the late mwalimu Julius Kambarage Nyerere of Tanzania was devoted to seeing Swahili used in various aspects of the country as soon as the country received its independence. Fortunately, he was not the only one who propelled the same idea; the late Dr. Kwame Nkrumah, the first President of Ghana, also made similar efforts. Maganda and Moshi (2014) state that:

> "In the early post-independence era, he was one of the African leaders who encouraged the adoption of Kiswahili as a continental language in order to promote Pan-Africanism. He showed his commitment to this call for Kiswahili as a continental lingua franca by championing directly or indirectly its adoption by some Ghanaian public institutions. These include Ghana Broadcasting Corporation (GBC), Ghana Institute of Languages (GIL), University of Ghana (UG) and SOS Herman Gmeiner College." (p. 178)

Nkrumah was joined by other African scholars, namely Wole Soyinka—a prominent writer; together, they began a quest for African unity with a proposal to make Swahili a common language for the entire African continent to promote Pan Africanism (Chebet-Choge, 2012; Maganda & Moshi, 2014). Other supporters of Swahili to become the African lingua franca included Ayi Kwei Armah, another African writer, and the late Professor Ali Mazrui (Katembo, 2008). The efforts to bring linguistic unity with a goal to usher Africa into greater economic and political harmony lacked support from the mass as well as African leaders themselves (Maganda & Moshi, 2014). In fact, such a task was possible if the leaders were willing, but instead, they seemed happy to continue using languages inherited from the colonial era until a glimpse of hope immerged from Tanzania once again.

To his credit, the late Dr. John Pombe Magufuli of Tanzania took simple but very practical steps to promote African languages. For example, he used local languages to greet and talk to people during his national campaigns; he sang with artists to the point that when he passed, many of them mourned him greatly because he was known to be the main supporter of the East African entertainment industry. In one of the leading national newspapers, the Standard, Stevens Muendo (2021) explains how Magufuli realized the power of language by making a bold decision to befriend Tanzania's youth through pop stars such as Diamond Platnumz, Harmonize, Ali Kiba, Hamis Mwinjuma, aka Mwana FA, Babu Tale, and popular actress and model Wema Sepetu, who in turn, were able to profit from their allegiance to his nationalistic political vision. Furthermore, in his call for structures to entrench Kiswahili in Tanzania's legal system, Mugarula (2021) explains Magufuli's efforts to bid farewell to the colonial language inheritance. He said, "It was dismaying that 60 years after independence, the Judiciary of Tanzania has continued to write and deliver judgments in English, which is a colonial inherited system." He stressed that "we must be proud of our own language; it is high time we use Kiswahili in delivering court judgments at all levels." As a result, efforts to translate all English-written laws in Tanzania into Swahili were made. On Monday, February 1, 2021 Magufuli promoted High Court judge Zephrine Galeba to be Justice of the Court of Appeal of Tanzania. This was after the judge carried a verdict in Kiswahili (Ndunde, 2021). Such action was a bold statement to highlight his perspective on the ability and value of Swahili in his beloved country of Tanzania.

The late President Pombe Magufuli with Diamond Platnumz
Image: Courtesy

Magufuli's efforts to promote Swahili did not end in Tanzania. After being elected chair for the East African Legislative Assembly (EALA), he made it possible for Kiswahili to be its official language, and for the first time, on September 15, 2016, he addressed the 17th EALA summit in Swahili. Thereafter, upon his election to become the chairperson of the Southern African Development Community (SADC), he advocated Kiswahili to become one of the fourth official languages. On August 22, he addressed the summit in Swahili for the first time (Mutethya, 2019). During his visits to Malawi, South Africa, and Namibia, Magufuli promoted the use of Kiswahili (SABC News, 2019). For example, he pledged to offer Kiswahili books and teachers to Namibia (Mumbere, 2019); and in South Africa, his efforts made it possible for the country to start teaching

Swahili in secondary schools and some higher learning institutions in 2020. He also offered to send Swahili teachers and teaching materials to countries such as Rwanda. To this date, "Kiswahili is already an official language in Tanzania, Kenya, and Rwanda and of the African Union" (Mutethya, 2019). By doing so, Magufuli started forming a new language ideology among his people of Tanzania and Africa.

Kiswahili has gained great momentum not just within Africa but also abroad. Asia, America, Canada, China, Europe, Germany, Poland, Japan, India, Mexico, and the Middle East continue to show great interest in Kiswahili. Consequently, in the United States, for example, Kiswahili has been "the most popular African language and a language of choice by both institutions and individual students who are interested in African languages" (Maganda & Moshi, 2014, p.202). International Academic organizations promoting the teaching of African Languages (ALTA), and Chama cha Ukuzaji wa Kiswahili Duniani (CHAUKIDU), a global organization for promoting Swahili, continue to strengthen the presence and spread of African languages in many institutions of higher learning. In the US alone, Swahili is taught in more than 130 colleges and universities, including in prestigious universities such as Stanford, Yale, Princeton, University of Pennsylvania, and Harvard (Maganda, 2020). Furthermore, based on popular TV shows and films, Swahili proves to be among the fastest-growing African languages in the U.S; its presence is also evident in the American public as people use Swahili words in simple conversations. For example, they say, "I am going on a safari," to denote intentions to travel but using the Swahili word "safari." Some say, "I love my mama," a Swahili word "mama" is used without the users realizing it is a Swahili word. In video games, Chinese American composer Christopher Tin composed a Swahili song in 2005 to be used for the game "Civilization IV" based on the Lord's prayer "Baba Yetu"—our father. The song was nominated for a Grammy award in 2010 in the "best instrumental arrangement accompanying vocalist's" category. In 2011, it was declared the winner in that category, making it the first to win as a musical piece for video games. In 2016, the US Navy performed "baba yetu" during the August memorial celebration (Kimuyu, 2016). Such linguistic shifts within Africa and abroad denote a new dawn for African languages, one that has the potential to alter how Africans think about their own identity when the world starts to show interest in what is African.

Language ideologies, therefore, allow us to understand how power and language are related. The connections between our thoughts about language and their ability to sustain power structures, which in turn allow those in power to continue their domination as social hierarchies, are reinforced through conscious and sometimes unintended acts of language use. For Africa, as Jillian Cavanaugh (2020) puts it, "Language continues to be a potent political weapon" (p. 56).

Therefore, with this poem, I call on you to imagine with me:

Imagine

Imagine a world
Imagine a life
Imagine a moment
Imagine a future
Imagine a possibility
Imagine a dream
Imagine a new beginning
Imagine African languages planted and
flourishing in the American soils
Imagine African languages becoming world languages
Imagine one day African languages louder and present
EVERYWHERE
Don't just imagine
Search, wonder, and then FIGHT

Discussion Questions

1. What is your language?

   _____

   _____

2. Is your language better than mine?

   _____

   _____

3. Do you think Africans should use their local/indigenous languages?

   _____

   _____

4. What are the advantages and disadvantages of Africans using their indigenous languages in their countries?

   _____

   _____

5. Is it important for Africans to use international languages such as English or French? If so, why and if not, why not?

   _____

   _____

6. Does it matter what language you value in your life? And do you think language plays a role in how you perceive your own sense of identity?

   _____

   _____

PART II

CULTURE

CHAPTER 3

COMPLEXITY
OF CULTURE

"The beauty of the world lies in the diversity of its people."
(Unknown)

IN THIS CHAPTER, I offer a working definition of culture, drawing from various disciplines. Presentation of key elements or characteristics of culture and how it is manifested through its various models will come next; thereafter, the various institutions that cultivate it are presented using specific and practical examples. Even more, I present ways in which the education system played and continues to play a great role in shaping the world's perspective on Africa and its cultural variances. Here, readers can clear out any myths regarding the true elements of African culture by examining the process that led to a distorted nature of African culture. This examination will allow us, in the subsequent chapters, to examine specific cultural elements and how they each illustrate a clear division between those that value and want to live in this world from an African way of life and those that wish to see those abandoned.

Before devoting time to the topic at hand, first, have you thought about how and why a total of about seven billion people on the face of this earth are different? How come we dress differently, talk differently, believe in different deities, and some don't even believe in any god? Some are regarded as poor while others are rich. Just stop for a moment and wonder why we as human beings do not have just one culture; after all, are we all not human? Well, genetic evidence supports that all people alive today have a common genetic material that can be traced to a sub-Saharan woman, later called African "Eve," who lived 200,000 years ago (Cann, Stoneking & Wilson, 1987). Linguistic observations by scholars such as Cavalli-Sforza, Piazza, Menozzi, and Mountain (1988) show a significant resemblance between the findings of Cann's tree of genetic relationships with the language groups that show all people have a common ancestry traceable to a group in Africa, thus all languages in the world having originated from Africa. By what method, then, did varied cultures develop?

Spencer Wells (2002) observes that possible changes in the climate and unclaimable pressure led people to migrate from Africa at different times. Those living along the coastal shores of southern Asia to South India to Australia are believed to have moved first; those who went to the Middle East went next, and from there, a group went to India while another went to China. The people who went to Europe through the Middle East are believed to have first passed through Central Asia and then scattered all over the world to other parts of America, Asia, Europe, and Russia. Antonio Damasio (2010) suggests that a long time of separation geographically simultaneous gave rise to various ways of understanding the world and how to relate to each other and those living in other environments.

Consequently, our complex worlds resulted in so many differences that made it necessary for some sort of social networks to regulate our survival, hence, the birth of cultures.

Meaning of Culture

These days, the word culture is very popular. Accordingly, if you search for it on google, you will get over six billion results, and a search using Google Scholar gives six million articles. Most social sciences and humanities consider culture to be very important. However, this concept seems to have also spread to other disciplines such as the arts and architecture (Baldwin, Faulkner, Hecht & Lindsley, 2006). Scholars indicate that no definition of culture is accepted universally (Wilhelms et al., 2009). From various disciplines, researchers define culture in different ways. Thus, even in this book, I will not try to provide a unified definition of culture as that would be a daunting task. However, I will highlight some definitions and concepts about culture critical to our discussion.

Culture derives from the Latin word "cultura," which implies the result of human interaction. I would say, in the most basic form, culture is simply the behaviour of a specific community that is learned and shared through human interactions. Hence, culture mirrors what people do within their societies. Over the years, many definitions were proposed, the first one being from Sir Edward Tylor. In his book, *Primitive Culture* (1871), he defined culture as "that complex whole which includes knowledge, belief, art, moral, law, custom and any other capabilities and habits acquired by man as a member of society." Following Tylor's lead, subsequent definitions were offered with additional ideas to the point that by the 1950s, Kroeber and Kluckhohn (1952) made a critical review of culture—concepts and definitions. They concluded that, at the time, there were 164 definitions. Among them was Robert Bierstedt (1970), who noted, "Culture is the complex whole that consists of everything we think and do and have as a member of society" (p.123). Meanwhile, George A. Lundberg and other scholars expanded that definition, explaining that culture is a system of a standard of judgment, belief, and conduct that is socially acquired and transferred, which, in turn, produce symbols and materials responsible for forming patterns and behavior.

In addition to their review, Kroeber and Kluckhohn (1952) also offered their own definition. "Culture consists of patterns, explicit and implicit, of and for behavior acquired and transmitted by symbols, constituting the distinctive achievement of human groups, including their embodiments in artifacts; the essential core of culture consists of traditional (i.e., historically derived and selected) ideas and especially their attached values; culture systems may, on the one hand, be considered as products of action, on the other as conditioning elements of further action" (p.181). According to S.I. Okita (1992), "[C]ulture or civilization, taken in its wide ethnographic sense is that complex whole which includes knowledge, belief, art, morals, law, custom and any other capabilities and habits acquired by man (sic) as a member of society," and thus "the cumulative knowledge of man (sic)" applies to all aspects of life in the historical context (p. 176). After sixty years, Taras (2009) noted that more definitions were still added. Another renowned scholar on culture, Geert Hofstede, defines culture as "the collective programming of the mind that distinguishes the members of one group or category of people from another" (Hofstede, 1980, p. 13; Hofstede, 2001).

Definitions such as the few highlighted above result in the following broad meaning provided by the Merriam Webster dictionary: "Culture is the integrated pattern of human knowledge, belief, and behavior that depends upon the capacity for learning and transmitting knowledge to succeeding generations and the customary beliefs, social forms, and material traits of a racial, religious, or social group;

(and) the set of shared attitudes, values, goals, and practices that characterizes an institution or organization." This definition shows the complexity of this concept. For most people, we understand culture to mean a society's way of life. Culture is the ongoing compromise of learned and patterned views, opinions, ideals, and manners. All definitions show that culture cannot be steady and static. Culture is "negotiated," which implies, certain ideas and patterns can be examined to better comprehend why a society is how it is. Because culture has patterns, it implies that there are identifiable similarities among people within a cultural group. The definitions also acknowledge that our beliefs of what is true and false draw from our cultural perceptions, thus our attitudes, including what we like and dislike, what we consider to be right and wrong, and how we behave, all depend on the makeup of our culture. These cultural elements form our identities.

Because culture is specific to its people, it can only be expressed efficiently and accurately by members of that culture. As a result, the possibility and speed of cultural change depend on changing social beliefs that shift based on preferences that ultimately change over time, based on environments and opportunities shaping interactions among people and historical experiences (Fernández, 2010). For cultural change to occur, it requires a process of endogenic intergenerational knowledge (Fernández, 2008). For this reason, it is important to offer clear guidelines that help a people articulate their own culture, which in turn will guide our discussion on why and how most Africans have lost their first love to their culture and what manifestations of culture substantiate a clear deviation from the original or authentic African culture? How can we claim foreign contact and historical circumstances such as colonization brought a different perception of the value and beauty of Africa? Such questions can be answered when we decipher specific characteristics that make up what we call "culture."

Characteristics and Models of Culture

I must acknowledge the debate about what should be characteristics of culture. In fact, such discussions can each be a topic of research (Minkov, 2012). Thus, my selection may not reflect all possible ideas, but rather, I highlight a few that pertain to my focus. Dan (2020) notes the following characteristics underscored by all scholars on culture. First, culture is "a complex multi-level construct. Second, culture is shared, meaning people of the same society share similar attributes, thus allowing others to expect, with some constraints, how specific people may behave (Andreatta & Ferraro, 2012). This projection is a testament to the third characteristic, that culture is patterned. Such forms can be seen in specific cultural items such as "rituals, daily routines, and habitual behaviours" (Dan, 2020, p.226). Such items shape people's perceptions of what is real and what is acceptable in a specific community (Bonder, Martin & Miracle, 2004). Fourth, culture is dynamic, though it takes a long time for changes to be manifested. Two processes are credited for cultural changes, internal changes—innovation, and external changes happening when a culture borrows from another-diffusion (Andreatta & Ferraro, 2012).

Fifth, culture is collective (Hofstede et al., 2010), meaning it is observed when practiced by a group of people. Thus, the sixth characteristic to note is that culture is learned within a specific context—it is not inherited. Seventh, culture is social, solely dependent on the interaction between people within their specific social settings (Hofstede et al., 2010). Thus, when two people are born in the same place and time but live in two different places throughout their lives, they will respond differently to various ideas. When people learn cultural aspects within a specific society, they go through a process known as enculturation (Lustig et al., 2006). Lastly, culture is symbolic, meaning specific aspects of culture stand for something else. For example, art, money but the most valuable and significant symbol of culture is language. Thus, devaluing a people's language allows for other forms of discrimination to take place. Elements are found in every culture, etic components, which convey the notion of cultural universality (Andreatta & Ferraro, 2012). Such elements are useful when cultures are compared (Triandis, 1994). On the other hand, emic components show the unique nature of each culture; thus, scholars use them when learning about a specific culture (Spencer-Oatey and Franklin, 2012). Therefore, every culture brings something different and unique to the world. Thus, "a culture seeks an identity and strives to maintain its individuality and distinctiveness while recognizing the fibers that connect them to other cultures in more subtle ways." (Colbert, 2010, p.17).

Therefore, it is important to identify the various fibers that display the uniqueness of each culture. According to Colbert (2010), there are "ten cultural characteristics that describe any group of people: (1) a sense of self or space; (2) communication and language; (3) dress and appearance; (4) food and feeding habits; (5) time and time consciousness, whether by time or age or status; (6) relationships; (7) values and norms defined by cultural needs; (8) beliefs and attitudes; (9) mental processing and learning defined by how people organize and process information; and (10) work habits and practices " (p. 18). These cultural elements help us see and recognize how we differ from other societies under the sun. However, how and to what extent are we able to recognize such features? The answer lies in examining different models of culture because each characteristic reflects cultural manifestation at a specific level within a specific context. Therefore, since the first characteristic of culture, as mentioned before, shows that culture is "a complex multi-level construct," researchers show the multiple levels of culture as well as "various levels nested within each other" (Leung, Bhagat, Buchan, Erez, Gibson, 2005, p. 362). As such, there are various models regarding levels of culture, such as a hierarchy model proposed by Pizam (1993), which posit that culture can exist at "supranational, national, industrial, occupational, corporate and organizational levels" and that every person fits in at least one of those levels (p.206). Erez and Gati (2004) proposed the top-down–bottom-up levels of culture, which considered the interplay within levels. They came up with five levels, namely, individual, micro-level, group culture, organizational culture, national culture, and global culture. Karahanna, Evaristo, and Srite's (2005) model contains six interconnected levels of culture: individual, group, organizational, professional, national, and supranational. Also, with six levels, Wilhelms et al.'s (2009) model is somewhat related to the two previous models. They include individual level, micro culture, meso culture, macro culture, meta culture, and global culture.

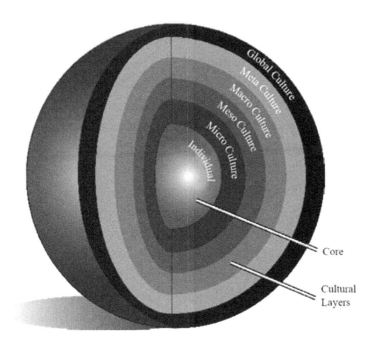

Figure 1: Sphere of cultural layers: standardized classification model
(Source: Wilhelms et al., 2009)

Dan (2020) explains,

> "a micro culture can be the family, the firm or a group
> of friends. A meso culture can be two or more firms
> or families, or the culture of a city, a state, an industry
> sector, or an occupation. The macro culture refers mostly
> to a nation or a country, but also, one can think about a
> national industry or an occupation on a nationwide scale.
> Meta culture refers to two or more national cultures or to
> some international organization (for example, the EU). All
> the examples mentioned before can become a global culture
> if they are examined on a global scale" (p.232).

The above-mentioned models show numerous levels of culture; however, at each level, other layers exist. Such tiers appearing within each element describe "the degree to which the cultural phenomenon is visible to the observer" (Schein, 2010). Several approaches have been proposed to illustrate such layers. First is the iceberg analogy proposed by Edward T. Hall (1989), which divides cultural components into two categories, observable (visible), also called surface culture; these represent the tip of the iceberg. For example, behaviour and practices, which can be seen. The other component comprises non-observable (invisible) attributes that are not easy to see and sometimes cannot be seen completely. These are also known as deep culture. They include attributes such as values, perceptions, beliefs and even attitudes. Another approach by Schein (1992, 2010) classed cultural tiers into visible and invisible. However, he went a bit further to create even finer items grouped in three levels. In the first level, things that can be seen, such as what people create, artifacts are placed here. In the middle, aspirations, goals, values, ideals, rationalizations and even ideologies are nested. The much inner level, third level, so to speak, hosts assumptions that people seem to take for granted.

Using a similar perspective but somewhat different approach, Trompenaars and Hampden-Turner (1997) came up with the "onion" idea using a diagram to illustrate various cultural elements within each layer. The first layer has products or artifacts such as language, buildings, shrines, markets, art, fashion and even food. Norms and values represent the second layer. These ascertain appropriate behavior—what is right and wrong, as well as what is good and bad. The diagram core contains unquestionable reality, the basic, unspoken assumptions often presumed to be there for no reason. Likewise, the Hofstede's "onion" diagram proposed by Geert Hofstede (2001) also shows the display of culture at different levels of intensity. The first layer of superficial elements of culture, such as symbols, which he defines as "words, gestures, pictures, or objects that carry a particular meaning that is recognized as such only by those who share the culture" (Hofstede et al., 2010, p. 8)—for example, how people dress, their flag, and even the language they speak. As a result, symbols can be copied, and the old ones replaced.

The middle layer has rituals, defined as "collective activities that are technically superfluous to reach desired ends but that, within a culture, are considered socially essential" (p. 9), and heroes thought as examples of good conduct in a certain culture, these can be imaginary people, alive and real or those that already passed away. The innermost expression of culture is placed at the core of the onion, which includes values, "feelings with an added arrow indicating a plus and a minus side" Hofstede et al., 2010, p.9). It is this core element that allows people to distinguish between good and evil or dirty as opposed to clean. Through various habits and traditions, people within a specific culture manifest these symbols, rituals, and heroes, which, in turn, allow people outside their cultures to observe such practices and label them as belonging to a specific culture.

Another framework by Spencer-Oatey (2004) following Hofstede's, Trompenaars and Hampden-Turner's models came thereafter.

This approach merged basic assumptions and values into one layer and introduced a new layer for social structures responsible for transmitting norms and values, namely systems and institutions. A third layer comprised of materials such as products and artifacts together with non-material elements such as behaviors and rituals were introduced. The last model by Rousseau (1995) consists of five layers, namely, artifacts, patterns of behavior, behavioral norms, values, and fundamental assumptions.

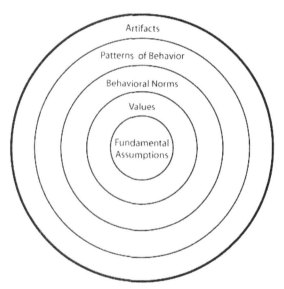

Figure 2: Layers of culture
Adaptation from Rousseau (1995)

As shown above, culture has been and will continue to be a contested topic. It is unlikely to see agreements among scholars regarding the meaning, characteristics, and even levels within each cultural element. Researchers proposed various models of culture using a bottom-to-top approach, some with six or five levels: the common ones being individual, group, organizational, professional, national, supranational, and global. Hereafter, I want to focus our attention on Spencer-Oatey's new cultural layer for social structures that aid the transmission of norms and values, namely systems and institutions. This is an important aspect because, as you will see in our later discussion, when a culture is no longer valued, it is critical to identify the cause; thus, examining how culture is transmitted will shed light on this aspect.

Transmission of Culture

Culture is learned and thus able to be perpetuated in any society around the world. There are no easy ways to pass culture from one person to another, generation to generation or one group to another, considering its complexity. Honestly, I asked myself a few questions, and you should too. Why do I respect elders and often find myself bending my knees a bit when I greet them? Why do I feel obligated to greet people, even strangers? When I talk to people, especially of the opposite gender, I tend to look down, I have a hard time looking people straight in their eyes, and the list goes on and on. As I think deeply, I am not able to pinpoint a specific class on proper ways to greet or relate to elders. No formal training happened, leading me to have the aforementioned behaviors for as long as I can remember. I am fully convinced that I learned these things without even thinking about them because they were passed down to me through daily experience within my own family and community. Little did I know that what I grew up believing to be the way to behave was so different from how others conducted themselves in similar situations. For example, when talking to my professors in American universities, without exceptions, all of them found it rude and a lack of respect when I looked down during our conversations. I remember one of them yelling at me, saying, "Look at me. You should be ashamed of yourself for not paying attention when I talk to you. Why are you not listening to me? Don't look down when I talk to you." With a soft voice, I said, "I am so sorry. I was taught not to look directly in the eyes of anybody, especially one older than me because it shows no respect and is a display of arrogance, like a statement of comparable status." I therefore do not plan to present all possible ways culture can be transmitted, but rather, I highlight a few that seem important regarding the topics at hand. Here, I underscore social structures, namely, institutions that facilitate the acquisition of culture.

Institutions are structures or mechanisms of social order; they govern the behavior of a set of individuals within a given community (Miller, 2010; Ludwig, 2017). Douglas North (1990) calls them "rules of the game," which shape human behavior in economic, social, and political life. He explains that institutions can be formal or informal with rules that coordinate social, political, and economic relations. Hodgson (2006) calls them forms of "established and prevalent social rules that structure social interactions" (p. 2). Drawing from the examples of my upbringing and my perspective and conduct regarding elders, I know I learned this, but it was not from a class. On the other hand, I have taught a class on various traditions, including ways to show respect to elders, and one of the ways was greeting them the way I grew up doing. Therefore, we can agree that institutions can be formal and informal. According to Leftwich and Sen (2010), "Formal institutions are the (written) laws, regulations, legal agreements, contracts, and constitutions that are enforced by third parties, while informal institutions are the (usually unwritten) norms, procedures, conventions, and traditions that are often embedded in culture," (p. 16). Sometimes the distinction may be hard because both types of institutions can "complement, compete with, or overlap with formal institutions" (Jutting et al., 2007, p. 36). Leftwich and Sen (2010) show that all institutions share the following characteristics.

- They are replicated through repetitive actions done by actors within communities.

- They offer an amount of assurance and reliability for everyday interactions between political, social, and economic relationships.
- They often stay the same for a long period of time, though changes can rarely happen and sometimes abruptly or in stages.
- They dictate behavior unconsciously, and those who act follow the unspoken rules without even realizing they are doing so.
- They shape behavior and thus influence performance and results from various actions.

A report by Research Programme Consortium on Improving Institutions for Pro-Poor Growth (IPPG) (2010) elaborates more on the role and nature of institutions in societies and among individuals. It shows that institutions do not determine what individuals or societies will do but rather shed light on predictable ways people within communities are likely to act. It states,

> "We all participate in a series of distinct but overlapping 'games' with institutions, or rules, at their core. Quite simply, human society is impossible without them. Effective institutions provide for predictable and stable patterns of interaction in all walks of life. So, institutions are thus best thought of as durable social rules and procedures, formal and informal, which structure—but do not determine—the social, economic and political relations and interactions of those affected by them" (p.15)

Therefore, to fully understand the interaction between individuals and other factors that influence ways people act within their societies to the point that others identify their ways as distinct from others, a closer look at three major types of institutions is useful in our discussion. Like most discussions on culture, when it comes to institutions, they can be categorized differently. However, following the previous body of literature, specifically Consortium on Improving Institutions for Pro-Poor Growth, I use three types of institutions, namely, political, economic, and social. Each type has a formal and informal category.

Political institutions are governmental systems that create, implement, and enforce laws. They are power controllers, dictating who gets the power, who uses it and who decides how to use it at all levels starting with national, regional, or individual level. This means decisions regarding societal issues such as rights, responsibilities, and privileges to obtain certain goods or services among citizens of a particular group or nation-state are all shaped by political institutions. They provide a way to represent interest groups and constituents by creating policies while reducing options. Political institutions exist to create and maintain stability by fulfilling three major functions, namely, integrating society norms, modifying various systems to attain common political goals, and protecting the integrity of the legal system from external dangers (Armingeon, 2016). Formal political institutions therefore have rules and laws at national and sub-national levels that govern ways to seek, win, control and even disseminate power. In other words, they give very specific information on the rules that govern how individuals are to play the political game within their states. The most common types of political institutions that exist around the world reflect the following categories:

1. Democracy: A system of government by the people; the majority rule by electing who will represent them—namely, eligible members of a state elected representatives.

2. Republic: A state in which supreme power is not inherited, but rather, the people and their chosen representatives chose a national leader, namely, president rather than a monarch.

3. Monarchy: A form of government in which one person inherits authority and reigns as a king or a queen.
4. Communism: A system of government in which the government plans and regulates the economy. It is a system organized around socioeconomic structures whereby goods are commonly owned, thus seeking to eliminate social classes.
5. Dictatorship: A form of government where power rests in the hands of a leader who makes the main rules and decisions with absolute power, disregarding input from others.

In most African countries, the formal governing bodies looked different before from the way they did after colonization. We will examine that aspect in the upcoming chapter. Likewise, communal problems were handled differently prior to and after colonial rule. Informal political institutions, on the other hand, have unspecified rules, unspoken regulations that somehow members of a particular group follow without a formal agreement. For example, in most nations, unspecified acts are expected from one who would be able to inherit political positions (Helmke & Levitsky, 2006).

Economic institutions refer to markets and industries handling the buying and selling of goods. These are systems that shape, promote and guide or sometimes even frustrate economic activity and development outcomes. Formal economic institutions make rules and guidelines that identify, classify, and establish the means and process to own property and start a business while directing ways to collaborate or compete with other stakeholders for economic success (Wiggins & Davis, 2006). Examples include banks, businesses, corporations, insurance companies, credit unions, limited partnerships, stock market, and trust companies. More specifically, in America, this would include the Internal Revenue Service (the IRS—the government tax-collection agency), the U.S. Federal Reserve (the government producer of money), the National Bureau of Economic Research (a private research agency). In Tanzania, examples include Tanzania Housing Bank (THB), Post Office Savings Bank (POSB), Tanganyika Development Finance Co. (TDFL), Diamond Jubilee Trust (DJT), National Insurance Corporation (NIC), National Provident Fund (NPF), to name a few. Informal economic institutions govern access to opportunities for economic gains. They include norms and acceptable practices based on social groups or gender; they are also responsible for implicitly excluding others. For example, an informal economic institution would be the caste system in India or the guanxi relationships among the Chinese in China (Wang, 2000). Both economic and political institutions, especially the informal ones, somewhat relate to social and cultural institutions.

Social institutions are groups of people united for a common purpose. They shape private and collective codes of conduct, dictate affairs and dealings between individuals, gender, and age-based social groups, among others. Therefore, many categories are identified under this group of institutions. The first and smallest social institution is the family. It defines affinity, which is a family member's blood or marriage relationship to another family member. This is the child's first introduction to society; it teaches children skills, knowledge about family and the community at large. Some examples of family institutions include the nuclear family (parents and children), extended family (relatives of parents and children), marital partners (husband and wife), monogamy (marriage with one partner), polygamy (marriage of one husband with more than one partner), polyandry (marriage of one wife to more than one partner). Family creates a sense of identity by connecting individuals with others by blood from generation to generation, thus, forming a family way of life, a specific tradition shared by all members of that social unit. Religion is another social institution that reinforces the norms and values of a society to help its members make positive contributions. Every human society has religion, although not everyone may have a religion. Examples of tangible items and groups include missions, temples, mosques, churches, taboos, monasteries, and totems.

Education institutions are another type of social institution, with the primary goal of passing knowledge and skills to individuals from one generation to the next by offering instruction that enables people to contribute to the wellbeing of their society. Formal educational institutions are places of learning whereby people of various age groups follow a systematic hierarchical structure involving subjects and a specified time of completion to attain certificates or degrees. Examples include preschools, childcare, primary (elementary) schools, secondary (high schools), and universities. Informal education institutions, on the other hand, provide practical learning often geared toward specific skills; they use diverse teaching and learning methodologies, local resources, are built on the learner's involvement, and use real-life learning examples.

There is a cyclical tendency within educational social institutions, whereby those working within them, such as teachers, professors, and even administrators, must be a product of the educational system themselves. These are the main engines that train and prepare society members for occupations for many generations. I must add, the above educational institutions are formal, but the informal education institutions are just as valid. They use other forms of instructing community members without necessarily having a defined period or a written curriculum. Thus, I turn our attention to ways in which formal educational institutions played a great role in altering Africa's perceptions about themselves.

Education Institutions and Africa's Cultural Revolution

The education system, through formal academic institutions, played, and continues to play, a great role in shaping the world's perspective on Africa and its cultural variances. To understand how this happened, let us take a walk down memory lane. Here, I focus on the approach used to educate Africans: I show two modes of instruction, formal vs. informal, and examine the content of the education offered, meaning what was taught and who benefited from it.

First, formal education did not recognize the inherent system already in place for many Africans to acquire knowledge; colonial powers instituted formal education through systematized academic apparatus, which used a Western approach that necessitated a new way of learning and new experts to make it work. Africans with knowledge about any content or skill without formal degrees or diplomas were regarded as "uneducated" and therefore unqualified to instill knowledge. Did Africans have no education system to instill knowledge and skills from one generation to the next to better their societies? The answer is no. Did Africans have the knowledge to help them navigate and even thrive within their environments? The answer is yes, although little is mentioned about innovations from Africa. Did Africans contribute anything great to their societies and the entire world in general? The answer is yes, but they are hardly recognized.

Let us begin with the education system. As mentioned earlier, prior to colonial domination, most African societies trained each other informally, meaning knowledge and skills were instilled through oral traditions as well as apprenticeship. For example, storytelling was a major way to instill values and knowledge but was also a form of recreation. Folktale orature was used to transmit cultural information and messages verbally from one generation to the next. In African societies, folktales serve as an essential means for documentation, education, and entertainment; they are deep-seated in African culture; they expound the cultural aspects of the community involving day-to-day life activities, whereby creating a sort of code of conduct for Africans (Heckler & Birch, 1997, Owomoyela, 2002; Insaidoo, 2011). Apprentice was another African mode of education. For example, the griots of West Africa are called different names in various communities. The Yorùbá people of West Africa call them Akewi Oba (the king's praise man) or Olohun iyó (golden voice). They are known to be the community's libraries, holding information about the history, resources, genealogies—including names of all related family members and many more. Ebine (2017) explains that the griots are found in Western Sudan and West Africa. They guard community history and re-create the tradition of oral performance. Generally, griots are found mostly in the Senegambia region, among the Manding, the Wolof, the Bambara, and other ethnic groups in the upper Niger region of West Africa from Mali to Niger. To ensure that knowledge is passed from one generation to another, those wishing to become griot undergo special training that takes years to master, but it is all done through an apprentice (Okpewho, 1992). To get a glimpse of the intricate nature of the griot, take some time to watch the film *Keita: The Heritage of the Griot*, which shows the nature and essential role of the griot in West African societies.

Second is content of education. Formal education sought to educate Africans about what seemed important for colonial powers to accomplish their agendas. The first approach was to use concepts divorced from African reality. By doing so, the African man started valuing what was not his. For example, in her Ted Talk, "How Africa can use its traditional knowledge to make progress," indigenous knowledge expert Chika Ezeanya-Esiobu shows how many Africans are facing identity crisis because they grew up learning about western education as the norm and the answer to the many problems that still run rampant in Africa today. First, she shows how at an early age, African children do not see the value in what they call home. For example, from a very early age, children learn using alphabet sheets with pictures and examples of items that did not match African reality. When teaching the letter "A," children learn "A is for apple." But what is an apple to an African child? It is a foreign fruit that only a few elite Africans can afford to buy because it is imported from abroad, thus expensive. The apple is not just some fruit but a representation of what the African man needs to understand. It shows him that hardly anything is valuable in Africa. Ezeanya-Esiobu elaborates,

> "A is for apple" is for that child in that part of the world where apples grow out; who has an apple in her lunch bag; who goes to the grocery store with her mom and sees red, green, yellow—apples of all shapes and colors and sizes. And so, introducing education to this child with an alphabet sheet like this fulfills one of the major functions of education, which is to introduce the learner to an appreciation of the learner's environment and a curiosity to explore more to add value . . . introducing education to me with "A is for apple," made education an abstraction. It made it something out of my reach—a foreign concept, a phenomenon for which I would have to seek the validation of those constantly and perpetually it belonged to for me to make progress within it and with it. That was tough for a child; it would be tough for anyone."

Also, African indigenous knowledge was not acknowledged and is rarely considered to deal with critical matters such as food security. For example, agricultural scholars who attend formal education are often not taught about effective irrigation methods suitable for the African environment regardless of their success. This reality is well reflected through well-documented research involving many failed attempts made by the World Bank and other agricultural funding agencies that sought to commercially irrigate large areas of the dry grounds of semi-arid countries such as Niger (IFAD, 2008). In a synthesis report titled "Investment in Agricultural Water for Poverty Reduction and Economic Growth in Sub-Saharan Africa," as well as Chika Ezeanya-Esiobu's September 2 (2014) post on Muslimscience forum titled "Traditional Farming Practices for Enhanced Food Security," shows an irrigation method practiced in a predominantly Muslim nation of Niger in West Africa known as Tassa. This method originated from the predominantly Muslim Yatenga province of Burkina Faso in the Sahel, whereby small pits were dug to reclaim land lost, or about to be lost, to degradation. By digging a grid of planting pits on very hard – rock textured – soil, Nigerien farmers increased the depth and diameter of the pits, added manure to the bottom of the basins that could hold water for an extended period, resulting in crops surviving severe drought.

Figure 3: Tassa (accessed from Muslim Science: Traditional Farming Practices for Enhanced Food Security Muslim Science (muslim-science.com)

Such knowledge was not shared with African children as they grew up, and in fact, many western methods are encouraged though they cost more and are not as effective. Chika shows that tapping into African indigenous knowledge such as the Tassa method has proven that "food security at the community level need not be founded on expensive and difficult-to-sustain, imported western technology."

Even more, the African child was taught to see westerners as heroes and knowledgeable about everything, including Africa itself. For example, like Chika, I grew up memorizing the names of westerners who discovered many landmarks in Africa. For example, Scottish explorer Mungo Park is credited for discovering the Niger River, although some villagers resided right next to the river and even used it in their daily lives. As Chika said, "Did it take a man from far away to show them a river that they grew up using? Not really." In my humble opinion, it would be okay to say that Mungo Park made the Western world know about the Niger river, but he could have also acknowledged and named the indigenous people who resided next to it. Even more, writing and publishing a book, especially in those days, was a privilege of very few, leave alone the language barrier that would have made it almost impossible for the world to know about discoveries made with indigenous scholars who spoke African languages. Let us consider, for example, if a Nigerian had written about it and wished to publish even a short article about the Niger river in his native language, would the entire world know about it?

Another explorer, Dr. David Livingstone, apart from the great Christian values that led him to fight against slavery in Africa and preach the gospel, the world knows very little of Africans who also played a great role and worked together with such missionaries for the same cause. Maganda (2008) shows extensively the role that Africans—Sukuma educators—played in establishing Africa Inland Mission (AIM) schools and spreading the gospel in Tanzania, such a role is critical and worth mentioning, but the world mostly credits foreign missionaries for such accomplishments. Dr. Livingston is also credited for discovering and naming Victoria Falls and becoming the first European to navigate the width of Southern Africa. I credit those who made it clear that he was the first European to make this accomplishment, but it makes you wonder how many Africans journeyed through the same trails with no mention of them. Please know that I am not lessening what Dr. Livingstone, Park, and many other explorers accomplished. I simply show how many African children like me grew up knowing more about the western world and their accomplishments but little knowledge of what our ancestors accomplished.

Therefore, the rituals, traditions, heroes, and even ways of learning that the African child grew up knowing were indirectly devalued. Without realizing it, it was easy for the African elite to slowly start looking down upon all that he believed to be true and important. His mind learned in a different way, the language that would usher him into a higher social status and make him a valued companion to the colonial master was foreign. The story did not end there. Soon after, many African countries received independence, the same systems set forth during the colonial rules continued, including education institutions and even languages of instruction. In the next chapter, let us take a closer look at two African indigenous cultures, namely the Sukuma of Tanzania and the Acholi of Uganda. This examination will give us a glimpse of specific cultural characteristics that distinguish one African community from the other. It also helps us start recognizing ways in which we can say when and how one specific people-group was made to think differently about the culture they once honored and placed great value on. The poem below captures the common portrait of Africa, signifying the battered attitude regarding Africa.

Portrait of Africa

Africa is dying
Africa is failing
Africa is perishing

Africa is vanishing
Africa is darkening
Because
Africans don't like themselves
Africans don't know who they are
Africans don't value what they have
Africans don't care about one another
You don't need to live in Africa to colonize Africans
You don't need to be white to enslave Africans
You don't have to know a lot to influence Africans
You don't have to use a gun to kill Africans
You only need to possess their minds

Resources for Further Explorations and Possible Questions

1. From your own perspective, what is culture?

   _____

   _____

2. Listen to the Ted Talk by Chika Ezeanya-Esiobu on How Africa can use its traditional knowledge to make progress: https://www.youtube.com/watch?v=28sa2zGgmwE&list =RDCMUCAuUUnT6oDeKwE6v1NGQxug&start _radio=1&t=1s
   Read more about Tassa Irrigation: http://muslim-science.com/traditional-farming-practices -enhanced-food-security/

   A. What surprised you about Chika's presentation?

   _____

B. What is your perspective about the use of foreign ideas to solve Africa's problems, particularly, food shortage?

_____

C. If you had to give a talk about this information another title, what would it be and why?

_____

4. Traditional Farming Practices for Enhanced Food Security – Watch the following clip:
   How I turn a profit on an acre of land | Emma Naluyima: https://www.youtube.com/watch?v=XytEhAzXdxo

_____

_____

5. Read the Synthesis report with various agricultural methods and interventions in Sub Saharan Africa: https://documents1.worldbank.org/curated/en/167991468303275116/pdf/437680SR0white10water0200801PUBLIC1.pdf

_____

_____

CHAPTER 4

EXAMPLE OF AFRICAN CULTURE

"The wind does not break a tree that bends"
(SUKUMA PROVERB AFRICA)

IN THIS CHAPTER, I present the Sukuma people of Tanzania to illustrate some features present in African ethnic groups. Please note that these characteristics are not present in each African society, but rather, they give a glimpse of possible elements that, though they may differ in some ways, help us see aspects of cultural features presented in chapter 3. I specifically chose the Sukuma because, as you will see later, it is one of the largest ethnic groups in Tanzania. But more importantly, I am a Sukuma. I feel better and confident to write about a culture I know first-hand, although I cannot claim to represent all that the Sukuma have experienced and can do. To this end, I bring a historical understanding of who the Sukuma are, their geographical location, population, occupation, marks of their traditions, and samples of what sets them apart. More specifically, I will give an account of stories that explain their origin. I intentionally spend more time on their economy prior to colonial rule to give the reader a feel for what it meant to be economically sound as a native African and to illustrate ways in which people's ways of life can be altered to the point that the world forgets their success prior to foreign contact. I later give a brief overview of one of the popular chiefdoms of the Wasukuma and later highlight specific features of the Sukuma people. In doing so, you will have a good foundation in understanding how such cultural features may be looked down upon or misunderstood by people outside the culture. Critical interpretations about Sukuma traditions will also be shared to give you a balanced perspective because though I am a Sukuma, I do not agree with every aspect of my own culture though I understand it and respect it.

Let me begin by saying that I love being a Sukuma. I am proud to be a Sukuma and I am grateful to be a Sukuma. I love being a Sukuma because growing up, I remember stories that my grandmother told me. I even witnessed in my own family that Sukumas are very hospitable. In the old days when transportation was scarce in many parts of the country, whenever passengers found themselves stranded due to bad roads or trouble with the bus or car, the Sukumas would welcome them in their homes, feed them, and the next day, give them roasted peanuts, corn, or cassava for the rest of their journey. I also witnessed this firsthand in my own family. My mom always cooked more food than we needed for each meal just in case someone came to join us, and indeed, most of the time, someone came. I love to share, and I believe it is because I grew up in such an environment. In fact, most of the time, I find myself making more food than I need because I always think someone will show up and I must have some food to give them. I am proud to be a Sukuma because hard work is a trait that marks our ethnic group. The Sukumas mean business; this was

EXAMPLE OF AFRICAN CULTURE ‖ 67

also reflected in the work ethics demonstrated by our late president Dr. John Pombe Magufuli's motto or slogan, "hapa kazi tu," "strictly business." Lastly, I am grateful to be a Sukuma because the Sukumas love unity and find ways to work together. Much of what I have just shared will be expounded more later. I must add, living abroad made me even more appreciative of how the Sukumas greet each other. The women kneel to greet elders and others of a higher status. Please do not judge me on this. I have come to appreciate this unique way of greeting elders, and I find myself doing so even in a foreign land. I do not remember anyone here in the US telling me, "Get up, please get up," but rather, they say, "Ohh! thank you. That is so special."

Sukuma greetings 1
Deodata Nkoswe and Misoji Mayala
Magu, Mwanza, May 28, 2021

Background

In a nutshell, according to Shayo (2016), Sukuma is the largest tribe in Tanzania. Many Sukuma live along Victoria Lake; their main economic activities are fishing, agriculture, and keeping livestock. Sukuma community is one of the communities in Tanzania which is still underdeveloped despite having many resources such as a lake, mining, and suitable land for agricultural production. The Sukuma ethnic group is among the tribes in Tanzania that still have a strong affinity to their traditional norms and beliefs. Both men and women abide and follow what they inherited from their ancestors. Below I give more details to this brief introduction of the Sukuma.

The word *Sukuma* means "north" and refers to "north." The Sukuma people are called Basukuma (plural) and Nsukuma (singular), and their language is Sukuma. The Sukuma area is called Busukuma. Generally, the Sukuma are believed to have migrated 400 to 500 years ago from the south part of Lake Chad; they belonged to the Bantu group. They travelled through the basin of river Congo and across Lake Tanganyika and later settled south of Lake Victoria. Among the 120 ethnic groups in Tanzania, the Sukuma are believed to be the largest group culturally and linguistically related to the Nyamwezi. The 1957 census shows the Sukuma to be about 1,245,908, while the 1967 census noted their population at 1,529,917, but their number has increased tremendously and is at 5.5 million to date (Hungwe, 2012).

According to Izumi (2017), the Sukuma are an agrarian society, meaning they are a community whose economy is based on producing and preserving crops and farmland; they mainly live-in northwestern Tanzania. In the 1970s, some of them began to migrate southwards in search of grazing land. They inhabited about 17,000 square miles to an area in northwestern Tanzania, south of Lake Victoria, during the Colonial era. According to Maganda (2008), "Their area covered the whole of Mwanza and Shinyanga and parts of the Mara, Kagera, and Tabora regions. Currently, Sukuma people also occupy large areas of the Rukwa and Mbeya regions" (p. 4), and their population has since increased tremendously as noted above.

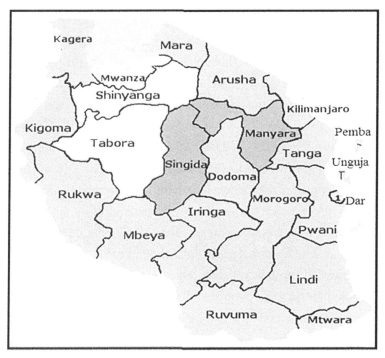

Figure 4: The sketch map of Tanzania, showing regions and Sukuma land
Adaptation from Maganda (2008). p.4

History of the Sukuma

There are differing accounts of how the Sukuma settled in their land. The Sukuma have many clans who claim a different story pertaining to their origin. However, the narrative most common and widely accepted is the one about Nkanda of the Mwanza region. I will give more information about this narrative later when exploring the concept of chiefdoms among the Wasukuma. Here, I present three possible explanations about the origin of the Sukuma people, also known as Wasukuma or Basukuma.

The first account claims several Sukuma dynasties entered the territory at different times; ancestors of the ruling family migrated and settled in the Sukuma land in the 17th century, but before then, the Sukuma land is believed to have been uninhabited (Abrahams, 1967). On the other hand, according to Per Brandstrom (1986), in the late 16th and 17th centuries, politically influential immigrants raided the proto-Sukuma/Nyamwezi speakers inhabiting Sukuma land and imposed ruling dynasties on them. In any case, the first settlers in Sukuma land were possibly hunters who later became agro-pastoralists, tending livestock and farming by the mid-19th century (Abrahams, 1967). Their occupational change is believed to have happened during European contact and once again in the late 1870s when they made cattle a major source of wealth (Birley, 1982).

The third account shows that the mainland of Tanzania, which was called Tanganyika, became a British mandate after the first World War. The Sukumaland, where the Sukuma resided and other rural areas in Tanzania, experienced expansion projects which were established to increase people and cattle population. For example, the population density of the core area of Sukumaland, namely the Old Mwanza District, grew significantly. It doubled between 1945 and 1988 (Meerterns, Fresco & Stoop, 1996) due to such expansion projects. In central Sukumaland, the number of domesticated cattle almost doubled between 1944 and the mid-1960s (Charnley, 1997) as well. Such growth resulted in a shortage of grazing land, prompting waves of Sukuma migration in the 1970s, which explains the establishment of the Sukuma society as shown through the following three major projects.

The first major product was the introduction of cattle plowing in the 1930s to increase agriculture production (Fuggles-Couchman, 1964). Second, the introduction of cotton as a cash crop from the 1940s until 1970 ushered Sukumaland into becoming a cotton manufacturing area (Hankins, 1974). Thirdly, the coming of tsetse flies caused a sleeping sickness, namely, African trypanosomiasis, prompting many eradication projects in Tanganyika to be carried out among pastoral people (Meertens et al., 1996). As a result, the Sukuma and the Maasai moved south to flee those insects. When Sukumaland became a big center for manufacturing cotton, a major shortage in grazing areas became a big problem as cotton fields became grazing areas. The Sukuma people tried to buy a lot of cattle to expand their pastoral livelihood, but the inadequacy of grazing land made these efforts unattainable (Birley, 1982). All of these happened before independence. In addition to the tsetse flies, in 1967, soon after securing independence from Britain, Tanzania adopted Ujamaa, a form of socialism that forced the Sukuma to live in the collective settlement promoted by Ujamaa policy (Galaty, 1988). Such a program was not favorable to the Sukuma, who wanted big pieces of land that would enable them to keep much livestock. Thus, in the 1970s, these factors led them to migrate southwards to search for grazing territory where the land had not been used (Fig. 5).

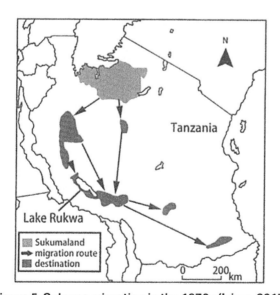

Figure 5: Sukuma migration in the 1970s (Izimu, 2017)

I tend to lean toward the third account of the Sukuma's migration because it gives a logical explanation regarding circumstances that led them to relocate and the aftermath of a new economic system that was not favorable to their agrarian lifestyle.

Economy

The Sukuma have a blended economy. Major economic activities include farming and raising livestock (Shayo, 2016) as well as hunting. By economic activities I mean, "conscious efforts using man's intellect and physical abilities which enabled them to harness nature in order to create material goods" (Kapinga, 2020, p. 35). Please note that all human societies, including the Sukuma, have always used any resources at their disposal, including economic, political, moral, and cultural, to meet their basic needs while aspiring to make advancements (Kapinga, 2020). Kimambo, Nyanto, and Maddox (2017) show that some scholars perceived pre-colonial societies inhabiting harsh environments with severe diseases and famine among others and could only gain a sense of security during the colonial era; on the other hand, the Merrie Africa approach established by Kjekshus (1996) shows pre-colonial Tanzania history characterized by an effectively functioning society with good governance. Koponen (1988) agrees that Kjekshus paints a good picture of pre-colonial societies showing they were well settled and able to control their environments using their own science to grow their population and feed themselves, thus living in harmony with nature before being devastated by natural disasters and economic mistreatment under colonial domination; this positive economic image is reflected among the Sukuma.

Pre-colonial and Colonial Economic Activities of the Sukuma

Generally, rain patterns, climate, and soil shaped pre-colonial activities among the Sukuma. Before colonization, the Sukuma were gatherers, collecting wild products. According to Benadeta Masawe (2019), during the rainy season, Sukuma women collected mushrooms of various kinds found near their homes, dug vegetable leaves from roots (Blohm, 1931), and collected insects such as termites to make one of the main foods. They dried these products to help them later when rain became scarce (Rodger, 1954). During the dry season, the men took weeks in the bush searching for wild honey and beeswax, which were in high demand among traders, although some contracted sleeping sickness during such long expeditions (Rodger, 1954). In this era, the Sukuma distributed their wealth throughout their entire community (Sugimura, 2011; Izumi, 2017). They maintained such economic independence through strong social networks based on the idea of reciprocity, whereby goods and services were shared and exchanged among relatives and within their neighborhoods or territories.

In the seventeenth century, during the rainy seasons, the Sukuma cultivated bulrush millet, maize, and sorghum. Rice was introduced in the 19th century; the Sukuma did not use it for consumption, but rather, it was used as an exchange commodity for goats, cattle, and sheep (Massawe, 2019). During this period, other types of crops for subsistence economy were also introduced, such as tubers: cassava and sweet potatoes, legumes such as chickpeas, beans, and groundnuts; these were all done on a small scale (Little, 1991; Hosea, 2018). The Sukuma also kept small animals such as ducks, chickens, guineafowl, and domestic pigeons, as well as big animals, mainly cattle. Gore and Kapinga (2020) show that cattle were used to pay dowry as bride price and was exchanged for grains to those who had food shortage. There was an uneven distribution of cattle among the Sukuma, which were used as payment for fines and other traditional fees. Generally, cattle were a status symbol and an important part of inheritance (Masawe, 2019, Abrahams, 1967). Other livestock such as goats and sheep were equally distributed than cattle. They were used for skin and meat, though they were sometimes used to pay court fines and bride price. Another major use of goats was during religious parties to honor ancestors; they were offered as sacrifices. On the other hand, special types of sacrifice called for the use of sheep (Malcom, 1953).

The Sukuma were also master traders in the pre-colonial era; they exchanged goods locally among themselves and societies nearby but also traded salt much further around Lake Eyasi in the northeastern part of Tanzania (Senior, 1938). In the northwestern areas of Bukoba, Karagwe and as far as Buganda and Katanga areas, the Sukuma carried trade activities as well (Kimambo et.al., 2017, Speke 1864). It is believed that the indigenous people in Sukuma land existed independently of others but to some extent competed with Arabs outside their local areas. For example, during the 19th century, Hosea (2018) shows the shore of Lake Victoria was used for long-distance trade through various caravan routes that connected with the ones established by Arabs and the Swahili coastal people. Every year, many groups of the Sukuma travelled from their local areas to East Africa's coastal states to meet with Arab and Swahili traders. Hosea (2018) continues to explain, Sukuma porters traded goats, oxen, ivory, and hoes in exchange for strings of beads, calico, gun powder, guns, copper wires, clothes, and other goods from Asia. Although waterways were also used for transportation, porterage was the main method of transporting commodities; consequently, many porters were employed by Arabs and the Swahili during the 19th century to carry imported goods from East Africa's interior towns and to carry back local goods obtained during the exchange (Ochieng & Maxon, 1992; Rockel, 1997). Floating rafts made of bamboo stalks or logs were also used for transportation in Lake Victoria. Later papyrus fibers were used to make more permanent rafts to stabilize them (Mingari, 1983)

In short, as expressed earlier, the Sukuma's economy is unique based on what happened historically. First, they moved and occupied a swampy land, which had not been inhabited before. Their farm animals allowed them to move from one area to another and cultivate based on their needs. The Sukuma are among agrarian societies in Tanzania and others from East Africa who were content with what they had; they did not wish to grow their economy (Kakeya & Sugiyama, 1985); in other words, they had no interest in large-scale farming (Sugimura, 2011). Second, the household was the basis for their large-scale farming, a feature shared by all pastoral societies. According to Izumi (2017), a Sukuma household is "a paternal family group that jointly manages a single budget, property, livestock, and land, under the supervision and ownership of the patriarch. A household is made up of an extended family that shares one or multiple homesteads . . . it is a unit of production" (p.58). Therefore, contrasted to families of regular farmers, the Sukuma's households tend to be extraordinarily large. Consequently, most Sukuma families need a large amount of labor to manage their production. The Sukuma did not employ laborers in the 1970s. They struggled trusting newcomers and laborers in general because they were often not dependable. They used to leave their jobs unexpectedly or steal anything around the house, including money.

During colonial rule, the British focused on infrastructure to gain access to places with raw material, namely cotton; thus, they developed a transportation system by marine, airways, railways, and roads to connect Mwanza town with other parts such as Shinyanga, Maswa, Musoma, and Kwimba. For example, in 1928, they completed building a railway from Tabora to Mwanza (Kimambo et al., 2017). The discovery of gold deposits 1920s and 1930s in East Mwanza, Mwadui, Musoma districts, and Southwest Mwanza gave Sukuma people major economic boosts. Mwanza town became a major commercial city by headquartering mining activities. Roads to the Geita Gold Mine and Mwabuki Diamond Mine played a great role in the major development of mining activities among the Wasukuma (Hosea, 2018). Roads improved communication between cities that facilitated cotton buying to reach designated ginneries such as Pambani and Salawe with the ones in Msalala Geita (Izumi, 2017). The Sukuma's participation in producing agricultural products, such as cotton, rice, groundnuts, etc., allowed them to buy other materials such as bicycles, radio, more cattle, take their children to school and roof their houses with iron sheets, and some were able to buy tractors as well as ox plows. However, the Sukuma lost the freedom to decide on what they wanted to do because the colonial masters dictated what economic activities should take place based on what was most profitable to them (Kapinga, 2020).

Sukuma Economic Activities during the Post-Colonial and Global Era

Tanganyika received its independence in 1961. During this period, the Sukuma society focused on increasing cotton production (TNA, File No. 19080). Consequently, the production of sisal, rice, and groundnuts decreased substantially (Izumi, 2017). During the 1960s and 1970s, communal mutual help groups (*Lubili or Luganda*) reduced labour costs among farmers with small farms. The Arusha declaration, which introduced Ujamaa villages changed Tanzania's economic landscape, particularly among the Sukuma. The Nyanza Cooperative Union, which oversaw selling rice, chickpea, and cotton, underwent serious losses during the period of villagization; production decreased sharply, dropping from 500 kilograms to 350 kilograms and even below because of poor cotton infected by pests and other diseases. Furthermore, moving peasants to the Ujamaa villages negatively affected agricultural activities among the Wasukuma (Masanja, 2019). From the 1980s to 2000, new irrigation methods were introduced, which led to increased rice production, making it a desirable cash crop over cotton. Thus, many Sukuma farmers switched to becoming rice farmers. Kapinga (2020) shows the complicated reality of the economic activities among the Sukuma during the free-market era. He writes,

> "In the early 2000s to 2010, the Cotton Development Fund was established as tripartite input-provision system whose main function was to supplement the prices of agro-chemicals and cotton seeds for planting. Under this regulation, smallholder farmers, ginners and the government were required to contribute part of their income to allow for the purchase of cotton inputs for the next season. This attempt failed because the ginners took advantage of the farmers' ignorance to exploit them. Furthermore, the problems related to the costs of inputs and labour continued up to 2010s" (p.43).

As explained, African countries, including Tanzania, experienced an economic crisis that led to structural adjustment programs (SAP), which were affected by the changing characteristics of the global market. Thus, the subsistence-based economy of producing only self-sufficient goods with no surplus declined due to a new dependency on the market economy. Even more, in rural households, there was an increased need to depend on non-agricultural employment for sustenance (Evans, 1991). Today, there is no shared possession of goods among the Sukuma communities, although it is still common among family members. A sense of interdependence, however, still exists and is a key feature of many Sukuma societies.

To date, when I visit my country, I see many villagers in Mwanza or Shinyanga areas working in big "*shambas.*" They work in groups, which consist of members from the same family, but often, they are "*lubili or luganda,*" communal mutual help groups, farming or harvesting to support a member of their community get the job done quickly and efficiently (Kapinga, 2020). Such groups are often not paid, but food is prepared for them. They pay each other mutually. Meaning, if you work on one farm today, next week, the group comes to help you. In the end, each family benefits when they collaborate with others. That is why I mentioned my love for the Sukuma, because no matter where the Sukumas go, when they find one of their own; they tend to bond and find ways to collaborate.

Even now, Sukuma people are the main cattle owners in Tanzania. Some families have very large flocks of a thousand heads or more, but many have smaller herds. The Sukuma still raise numerous types of livestock, such as sheep, goats, cattle, and donkeys. Except for donkeys, which are used for transportation, the rest are reared for food, as had been done in the pre-colonial era. The Sukuma continue to value cattle, and you may wonder why. Izumi (2017) explains,

> "Cattle have many uses in Sukuma society, and are cultivated for various purposes, as explained . . . People only milk cows, and their milk is used not only for food but also for many rituals, as well as for sale . . . Beef is eaten when households have important rituals and guests. After slaughtering cattle, Sukuma make their hides into many useful items, such as rugs and rope. Furthermore, cattle are the most important exchange for goods such as bride wealth, and they function as significant media that make and maintain households' social relationships. Cattle are the most important property and a symbol of wealth in their society, so a man who has more than a thousand cattle is called '*nsabi n'taale,*' with reverence. This means "a man of great wealth" in the Sukuma language" (p. 61).

Therefore, wealth among the Sukuma is still based on the number of cows a person owns. However, the Sukuma people mainly rely on subsistence farming of the following staple crops, some of which have been cultivated since years past: millet, sorghum, rice, sweet potatoes, and corn (maize) in addition to cotton and tobacco as a cash crop. From my own experience, I also know many Sukumas who also grow some vegetables, fruits, groundnuts, beans, and most people have cassava planted around their houses or in their fields. Most families grow food for themselves and attempt to produce some surplus for the market. Although hoes are still used by most families, some use plows pulled by oxen, but richer people hire tractors to cultivate large pieces of land. According to Izumi (2017), Sukuma's economy, like other East African peasant economies, focuses on producing just enough to sustain themselves by mainly depending on family labor, which is why they also use other means to earn income, including commercializing their farming. Although they did not like to employ laborers, in recent years, large households tend to employ many of them because family members can monitor them (Izumi, 2017). They realized that the size of the family correlates with the amount of labor, which in turn dictates how large or small their production would be. Additionally, several wealthy Sukuma people focus on various types of businesses and own shops in local villages and towns, while others have big businesses, including transportation around the country.

In all, the Wasukuma produced what they needed to survive and flourished in their environment before colonial rule. Their economic activities had to shift from making what they needed for their sustenance to producing what the colonial masters demanded. The colonial policies forced Wasukuma to produce non-food cash crops such as rice and cotton. Unfortunately, the post-colonial era inherited a similar economic system set in place during colonization. Although some changes were attempted, the will and even capacity to bring back sustainable economic development among the Sukuma communities were not realized. Wasukuma keep trying on their own to win the poverty battle, which continues to rage to this date but make no mistake, some of them are wealthy on their own merit.

Political, Social-Cultural, and Other Traditional Features
History, Role, and Status of Sukuma Chiefs

The Sukuma area was organized by chiefdoms following the migration of various groups believed to be Basega, Balongo, Bangolo, Babinza, and Bakwimba, who consolidated the sparsely inhabited areas around Lake Victoria. With impressive skills, strength, and power to cut down trees and clear the bushy areas they found, they had undeniable leadership abilities that led them to be crowned leaders—chief over their groups. The word *ntemi* in Kisukuma comes from the verb *Kutema*, which means to cut down many trees or clear a thick bush by literally cutting it down. The person who clears out bushes or cuts down trees is *ntemi*, a role signifying what the leaders did when cultivation season started, but this could possibly denote the chief's role of cutting down arguments that came after heated discussions among elders in the village (Pambe, 1978).

Based on oral history, chief Muletwa of the Lushamba kingdom guided his son Nkanda to travel from Nyalukalanga in Geita District to a place between Magu and Bujora, an area near Magaka and Kinango (Hinkkanen, 2009). Upon arrival, Nkanda said in his native language, "Lnye Nsukumala aha," meaning let us rest/camp or stay here. This is where the term Sukuma was first heard and thereafter developed into the cultural group we now call Sukuma. Ultimately, the indigenous group inherently present when Kanda arrived, namely, Waruli, invited him to become their chief because they believed he had medicine that made people fear him. They also believed he could protect them against crocodiles that broke their fishing nets, and more importantly, he had the ability to make rain. Knowing it was against the customs of his people, the Bazinza and Balongo, Nkanda declined the offer because a leader was to be a descendent of the chief from the matrilineal side. Nkanda then traveled back to his village, where his father appointed his sister Minza's son to lead the region where he was welcomed to rest the first time he arrived. Thus, the current fifty-two Sukuma chiefdoms are believed to have been established from the first Sukuma chiefdom still recognized as Nsukumale (Sukumalaha).

Another version of this tale posits that Ilembo of Nyalukalanga went to Seke searching for game. He invited his sisters who became leaders of Sukuma, Ng'wagala, and Ntuzu, and among them was Minza. Then Nkanda became a military leader of Ilembo after marrying Minza and forcibly united several local groups militarily. No one knows which tale is true, but one thing is for sure, Nkanda holds a significant place among the Sukuma because nearly every Sukuma clan traces its lineage and chiefdom back to him; and shows why the Sukuma blacksmiths from the Babinza and Balongo clans hold a significant place in forming the identity of the Sukuma (Pambe, 1978).

Archival photographs of Masuka, the Ntemi (chief) of Mwanza Chiefdom in his regalia, c. 1900. Courtesy of the Archives of the Missionaries of Africa, Rome.

Minza no doubt held a prominent position among the Sukuma either as a wife, sister, or mother of Nkanda. As a result, Sukuma is matriarchal in clan lineage and naming system (more on naming later). Furthermore, when Wasukuma greet each other traditionally, they identify and honor their lineage to their chiefdom. For example, those related to one of the major chiefdoms of Sukuma Babinza greet each other in the name of Minza. Thus, their greeting is referred to as Iminza, referring to Minza herself or her family. In response, a person mentions the name of his or her grandfather, referring to the ancestral connection to original chiefdoms. Likewise, every Sukuma is connected to a specific chiefdom, and during greetings, they ask each other the name of their lineage. In doing so, the Sukuma signify the importance of Sukuma loyalty, which played a significant part in making sure people do not marry within their own clans (Bessire, n.d., Hinkkanen, 2009). Below, see a sample of Sukuma greetings reflecting the chiefdom. Below see photos of girls kneeling when greeting elders.

Iminza . . . . .Term of respect and mother of the first Sukuma Chief.

Ng'wa nani? . . . . . .What is the name of your family?

Ng'wa Fumbuka. . .Fumbuka (Sukuma family name-founder Sukuma Museum).

Uli mhola? . . . . . . .Are you at Peace?

Nali Mhola. . . . . . .I have Peace.

Sukuma greetings 2
William Bubele & Janet
Magu, Mwanza,10/28/2021

Sukuma greetings 3
Susana Mchembe & Tabitha
Ngogo, Mwanza, 10/30/2021

Sukuma greetings 4
Eva Enoka & Ng'wamba
Ngogo, Mwanza, 10/30/2021

Many people who have lived with the Sukuma for a period understand and testify that the Sukuma love peace, *mhola*. Apparently, this stance was established during the chiefdom era, whereby a chief's power relied heavily upon his ability to control and maintain a state of *mhola*. The word *mhola* comes from a Kisukuma verb *Kuhola*, which means to thrive, to be healthy and is part of everyday Sukuma greeting as shown above. It is also believed that, as in Nkanda's story, chiefs have some magical powers based on their connection to ancestors and gods. Accordingly, chiefs were to reveal such semi-divine powers or magic during ceremonies that occurred when twins were born, before battle, annual agricultural cycle, or enthronement (Reid, 1982). The following ceremonies were specifically designated for a new ntemi during the precolonial era:

1. Kundima – Apprehending of the candidate
2. Kugundika – Seclusion and lessons from banang'oma on how to be chief
3. Kung'wanila Ntemi – Enthronement

Governance and Leadership

According to Hinkkanen (2009), members of the royal family, also known as banang'oma, chose the next chief among daughters of previous chiefs. These cabinet members also trained the new CHIEF. His leadership heavily relied on banang'oma as well as other advisers, known as wanangwa: bafumu, diviners, rainmakers, traditional healers (Waganga in Kiswahili), who advised him based on their expertise (Jangu, 2012). The Balongo or blacksmiths who made weapons, agricultural tools and controlled fire were also part of the chief's advising cabinet together with the bafumu; they were to ensure peace, and if *mhola* is not experienced, they were punished for either poor predictions or advice that brought adverse reactions to the Ntemi (Machangu, 2010). These intermediaries would usually take the blame if *mhola* was challenged and would be punished for mistakes such as poor predictions or bad advice that misled the Ntemi. By doing so, the chief was shielded from criticism unless problems continued for a long time, then he would be dethroned.

Sukuma traditional diviner (*nfumu*) dancing to perform a ritual
Photo Accessed from:
https://kwekudee-tripdownmemorylane.blogspot.com
/2013/03/sukumapeople-tanzanias-largest-tribe.html

Apart from the leadership, there was a direct relationship between the chiefs to spiritual and economic prosperity. First, the chief owned the land, and anyone with land belonged to him in Sukuma land. No one was allowed to sell land, although those who cleared the bushy areas themselves were allowed to lend it to others as well as let their descendants inherit it (Izumi, 2017). Second, community members gave tribute to the chiefs who facilitated trade and controlled who and how fire was used by the blacksmiths-balongo. According to Pambe (1978), notions of "medicines" "spirits, spirit of ancestors, and spirit possession," are critical to any rituals and power because they are believed to give a person ability or special powers, and they therefore play a great role in making a chief. As such, the chief's ability to communicate with their ancestors signified his strength to keep his chiefdom safe and prosperous. Therefore, making fire, spearheads, and hoes (done by the blacksmiths: balongo); producing traditional medicines (done by traditional doctors); creating mhola and rain (done by the chief) formed intricate, emblematic—yet sacred—authorities vital to the welfare of the Sukuma society (Bessire, n.d.). During royal ceremonies, sacred objects called *shitongelejo* were passed down through ancestral lines. A chief would always have such items from his predecessor and ancestors; these are to be interpreted carefully because they differ from one chiefdom, clan or even family. All of these were possible before and during the colonial era.

Sukuma royal drum from Sukuma Chiefdom, Royal Pavilion, Sukuma Museum

Isumbi lya itemelo, or royal throne, said to be 400 years old. Owned by Ntemi Mbilingi of Sukuma Chiefdom, Royal Pavilion, Collection of the Sukuma Museum, Bujora village

Machangu (2010) elaborates, the chief's influence started to diminish during the colonial period because it came from the influential colonial government, thus losing its relevance to traditional authorities. Chiefs became a part of the colonial hierarchy and no longer involved their people in decision-making, hence allowing the British to rule indirectly. This strategy allowed the colonial administration to purge out customs and native law by making the chiefs civil servants. Consequently, they were unable to preserve their authority and lost their economic and spiritual power. Machangu (2010) continues, the chief's association with colonial rule and their lack of leadership to support the national movement to fight for independence tainted their image among governmental political leaders. Therefore, the day before independence, the then-political leader, mwalimu Julius Kambarage Nyerere, made the following statement regarding the chiefs: "We tell the chiefs frankly that their authority is traditional only in the tribes, Tanganyika is not a traditional unit at all, and if the chiefs want to have a place in this thing we call Tanganyika, they have got to adapt themselves to this new situation, there is nothing traditional in the central government of Tanganyika" (Bessire, n.d.). Since the chief's authority would no longer transcend traditional lines, in 1961, the year Tanganyika received its independence, the Sukuma Federation of chiefs was extinguished and thus eliminating the chief's political power. During that transformational time, many chiefs still wore their royal regalia, but most of them were forced to hide where the environment and nature caused their destruction. Although things have changed among the Wasukuma, currently, many chiefs are actively involved in their communities and continue to participate in various traditional ceremonies. The most popular ceremony still practiced today where chiefs are actively involved takes place at the onset of the planting season. It is called *Busunzula*—shaving of the chief's hair.

Today, chiefs are connected to kinships within various Sukuma clans. By kinship, I mean social relationships that form a network of important people in a person's life within a specific community. Thus, major kin groups in a specific Sukuma society are descendants of former chiefs, although others come from leaders who used to hold political offices as elected government officials. The most important part of kinship is facilitating and maintaining interpersonal relationships within and beyond family lines.

Family and Marriage

There are two major categories of marriage among the Wasukuma, those with bride-wealth and the ones without it. When a husband pays the bride price, he gains rights to all the children bore by his wife (Makoye, 2013). If some of the children are daughters, he has the right to get the bride-wealth given for them, but, in turn, he is responsible for paying for his sons and is obligated to provide an inheritance for them. Historically, the bride price was a great way to ensure marriages are taken seriously and relationships between the bride and groom are sustained accordingly. The major form of bride price among the Wasukuma are cows, but the amount differs significantly based on various criteria. One of the criteria was color. The more light-skinned you are, the more the cows your father receives. Another criterion is level of education, the more educated you are, the more cows your spouse pays. My husband said he was glad to have paid the bride price before I got more educated!! I always tease him to give my father more cows! To which he replies, "I think I have given him more than the number of cows I could add. After all, I love you. I think that is more important than the cows!" The cows often don't stay within the father's household. They are often divided among the elders in the family. Consequently, when the husband and wife have marital problems, the senior family members counsel the couple with hopes to rescue the marriage and avoid giving back the cows. However, according to Shayo (2016), so many fathers feel pressure to keep the cows even if a daughter is being mistreated. One male explains,

> "Bride price used to have great value to the parents, when a bride price is paid for a girl the whole clan celebrates, and so, even if the son-in-law misbehaves, the clan cannot do anything. Even if the daughter is mistreated, you as a parent cannot do anything because of the property or livestock that you were paid. But these days things are a bit different. In those days a father was proud to have wealth even if his daughter is being mistreated, he would ask her to be tolerant" (Shayo, 2016, p. 44-45).

Some Sukuma women have felt the negative side of bride-wealth marriage. One states, "Paying a high bride price gave the man an excuse to mistreat the woman, and the father could not return the cattle, and therefore the woman continues to be mistreated by her husband and she won't have anywhere to go" (Shayo, 2016, p.45). Another female added,

> "By not paying a bride price, women won't be mistreated, even now you can see that there is a difference between women who were married without bride price, and the women for who bride price was paid. The ones for whom bride price was paid tend to be mistreated because they are afraid of being divorced and this leads to adopting a certain behavior because they won't get any assistance from their families because they already took the bride price" (Shayo, 2016, p.45).

Therefore, bride price has its advantages and bears great significance among the Sukuma. On the other hand, it has negative aspects, as shown above. The act of paying the bride price before the marriage takes place is called *gulunja*. This is commonly done in most prosperous areas where families have cattle. The marriage without bride-wealth, on the other hand, has its own drawbacks. The father has no rights to the children, thus, letting maternal kin decide how much the husband will pay for each child if he wishes to keep them or to have any rights over them. The amount is often larger for daughters than sons. The act of paying the bride price after a child was born to a non-bride wealth marriage is *gukwa*. Marriage is described using active and passive voice, signifying who initiates and who responds. Thus, the man initiates marriage or proposes, he marries, and thus the verb *kutola* is used, while a woman is married, thus the verb *kutolwa* is used.

After marriage, if bride-wealth was paid, the married couple lived with the husband's family (patrilocal residence) but eventually, the sons moved away. Neolocal residencies whereby married couples live together in a new residence have become more common. To date, polygamous marriages are still practiced among the Sukuma, but they seem to be unstable in most cases except with older men or chiefs. Marriages with bride-wealth seem to be more stable, but divorce is more frequent for non-bride-wealth marriages. Within a household of one or multiple wives, a patriarch takes leadership of that family. Izumi (2017) explains,

"A patriarch has strong rights to his property . . . Although daughters leave their parents' household when they marry, sons usually remain there for a long time. Even though sons do have the right to inherit their father's property and become independent when they first marry, sons who have multiple wives and children typically remain in their father's household. Therefore, in the Sukuma society, a household tends to increase in size and rights to property tend to be concentrated in the person of the patriarch" (p. 58).

Pertaining to the division of labor, generally, men do most of the heavy tasks, which tend to be shorter, while women do more repetitive tasks. Men are expected to tend cattle. Often boys take them to graze in the plains or somewhere around a communal grazing land. In the dry season, they also graze in woodlands. Historically men used to hunt, do ironworking, and anything regarding making or fixing machinery. On the other hand, women focus on pottery, fetching water and firewood, cooking, caring for children, and other household chores such as doing laundry or sweeping around the house. Both men and women farm and do the harvest. Although the Tanzanian government has made land-ownership policies giving men and women equal rights to own land, this has proven to be challenging among Wasukuma as land is often owned by the family patriarch, as mentioned earlier (Izumi, 2017; Shayo, 2016). In fact, only sons of bride-wealth marriages, or redeemed sons, have the right to inherit wealth such as land. In turn, they are to look after their daughter's needs as well as the rest of their siblings, especially sisters. Unredeemed children are vulnerable to having no inheritance from either their father or their mother's kin.

Special Sukuma Traditional Features
Education, Entertainment: Singing and Traditional Dances

The Sukuma revere ritual and tradition yet continuously adapt, modify, and redefine their ways of life. In fact, as Jangu (2012) notes, "They inspired the richest colonial literatures on ritual anywhere and prompted missionaries and other "educated people," early in their introduction, to found museums dedicated to Sukuma cultural practice. The Sukuma people have always fit uneasily and yet productively within the Tanzanian state" (p. 19). In the past,

"Sons, grandsons, parents and grandparents convened before shikome (a site outside the house with an open fire where male family members met). This was a place where culture, tales, riddles, and legends were told. The gathering was usually held during the night as a relaxation mechanism after a day's work. Plans for the next day's work were also disseminated during these meetings. Sukuma cultural values were shared among older and young generations during these evening gatherings. In modern Sukuma society, however, this cultural system is disappearing due to new and widely propagated forms of education, modernization, and the globalization (Jangu, 2012, p. 21).

Throughout Tanzania, the Sukuma are well known for their singing and special dancing styles. Songs and dances are another part of the Sukuma's way of teaching and inculcating societal ideals throughout generations. Singing is done through various forms such as oral poetry, whereby composers write short or long songs to be sung in various venues and occasions such as wedding ceremonies, death, childbirth, while others are taught to singing groups like choirs to be shared in public places. There are many religious singing groups in the Usukuma areas, many of which I know and grew up listening to, for example, Mwanza Town Choir, AIC Makongoro Choir, AIC Shinyanga Choir, AIC Dar es Salaam Chang'ombe Choir, Neema Gospel Choir, AIC Chang'ombe, AIC Nyakato Choir, and many more.

In addition to the above singing groups, traditional dances are integral among the Sukuma. It is believed that cooperative farming groups, which are also called "reciprocal village labor," that moved from farm to farm to assist one another to till farms established such dancing groups. For example, the Tanzania Sukuma, Bachonga Magembe is one of such groups that use a group of young men to work in farms; one member plays a musical instrument while others work following the rhythm and speed of the song and music instrument. It was during such a long day of work when workers needed to maintain their energy and pass time and thus composed songs and lifted their hand-held hoes following song and drum rhythms. Today, such tradition continues involving new innovative dances performed in annual competitions transcending farm work (Jangu, 2012). For example, the Tanzania Sukuma Jeshi Dance specializes in imitating a military scenario using the dancers to showcase various maneuvers of gun battle.

Bugunda ya Ntulya: Sukuma traditional dance group
by Fabian Mhoja (February 18, 2016 for Sukuma Museum Bujora)

The dance competition in Usukuma takes place during the summer months, June to August, when people do not need to work on their farms. National holidays such as Saba saba, July 7, and Nane-nane,

August 8, are the major dancing festivals commemorating farming and work. These dance competitions started with two Sukuma dance societies: the Bagika and Bagalu that began in the mid-19th century. Their lead composers and dancers, Ngika and Gumha, lived with traditional doctors to learn powerful medicines and were therefore challenged to compete to show who had the most potent medicines. People followed whoever they believed was most powerful. Ngika led the Bagika society while Gumha led the Bagalu. These societies still have followers and continue to compete each year during dance competitions.

Another dancer currently famous among the Usukuma is Maganigani, he uses contemporary innovations and dances sogota, which features red and white designs of thigh-high multicolored shorts, shirts, and socks. Additionally, the Sukuma have other dances such as the bugologolo and the snake dance. They also hold other series of dance competitions in the months of June through September known as "wigashe" (pronounced: wee-gah-shay). These are groups of various songwriter composers known as *mlingi* in Sukuma. These are called wigashe because the leaders stand but the rest of the group sit in log benches surrounding the singer. When the composer sings, the chorus echoes the same words following the given rhythm. Wigashe

Wigashe Sukuma dance: Sukuma Museum, Mwanza—Bujora

composers write special lyrics that range from national elections, Sukuma history, advice on good moral conduct, and warning to avoid contracting sexually transmitted diseases such as AIDS. Some compose about major events, such as Budelele, whose song in June of 1996 memorialized those who died during the ferry accident in Mwanza.

Apart from Tanzania, Sukuma dances have transcended national boundaries to other parts of the world, particularly Denmark, which has lively intercultural interchange with the Sukuma. This began in the late 1960s when many Danes visited Usukuma areas such as Bujora and fell in love with Sukuma dancing and developed close relationships with many Sukuma communities. Therefore, Danish groups visit Usukuma yearly to experience the culture and practice dancing. Each year Danish groups continue to visit Usukuma to practice dancing and experience Sukuma culture; such a relationship resulted in many dance groups in Denmark, and they continue these exchanges to date. Examples of dance groups birthed from this Sukuma-Danish cultural relationship include the Utamaduni ("Culture") group, Watoto na Wengine ("Children and Others"), Ikumbo ("Whip"), and Kisiwani ("Of the Island"). Each year, Sukuma dancers are invited by these groups, and a weeklong Sukuma cultural camp is held often at the end of July. A group of Danish people learn Sukuma dances and perform. For example, at the end of the Eliza workshop in 2016, a dance was performed reflecting Danish and Sukuma collaboration. Consequently, some Sukuma dancers have stayed permanently in Denmark. Also, Danish artists such as Manongu collaboratively sing and dance with Sukuma dancers as in the song Ung'wana undololo uyu. Currently, Sukuma artists such as Bob Haisa compose songs and incorporate community members to dance. One of the famous songs often performed among the Sukuma during "*kulunja*," paying the bride pride, is "bhatoja." It is an example of the amazing combination of the Sukuma singing and dancing while catering to traditional and modern aspects of entertainment.

Traditional Medicine and Social Justice Organization

To say that traditional medicine is an important part of the Sukuma people is an understatement. I cannot present all there is to say about Sukumas traditional medicine; however, here are a few aspects to highlight. Most Wasukuma depend on local traditional medicines. Thus, they pass such knowledge from one generation to the next using oral communication; even after the introduction of modern medicine and hospitals, most living in rural areas cannot access such facilities and, in many cases, they cannot afford them (Vats & Thomas, 2015). The Sukumas believe in supernatural powers and often seek help from *"Bafumu"* diviners, *"Balaguzi,"* medicine men, and *"Basomboji,"* soothsayers. According to Backhaus (2003), Sukuma diviners shape their medical system, including the physical landscape, based on cultural conditions and surrounding materials that are easily accessible and grow wild in surrounding environments. Jangu (2012) elaborates that Sukuma healers' residential premises are "surrounded with a fence of *mnyaa* (Euphorbia tirucalli L. plant) or shrubs for privacy and security. Other healers opt for stones to surround their premises. Their houses are of the msonge (round) type, particularly their treating rooms. Roofs are made of thatch but also have lupingus (shells collected from the ocean) and snail-shells on top" (p.404).

With such distinction of their landscape, Wasukuma and others in Tanzania can identify a healer and go for treatment. Others also specialized in predicting when rain would come or to council the chief accordingly if there was a drought (Izumi, 2017). It is believed that among the Wasukuma, people tried hard not to anger the rain specialists in fear of causing drought in the area (Vats & Thomas, 2015). Other types of medicine are given for various matters such as helping a woman conceive, attracting wealth, and helping someone

A healer's compound surrounded by Mnyaa plant
(Jangu, 2021, p. 404)

win in competitions such as dance. Additionally, other medicines were given to traditional soldiers: namely, Sungusungu, to get rid of timidity and fear. Below I give a brief overview of the Sungusungu.

According to Heald (2002), all sources show that the Ugandan war of 1979 produced a surplus of guns and left many young males without jobs. As a result, the increase in cattle thievery led to the emergence of grass-roots law and order organizations known as Sungusungu in 1982. This movement started among the Sukuma, in Kahama District of Shinyanga Region, Central Tanzania. Before long, the organizations started punishing other crimes such as witches, run-away wives, adulterers, and those who failed to pay their debts (Mesaki, 1995). The organization started in one or two villages whereby charismatic leaders were chosen to manage villagers using a hierarchy leadership style starting with a chief (ntemi), chairman (mwenyekiti) and a secretary (katibu). Sungusungu spread from Sukuma societies to other parts of the country, such as Rukwa, within a year. Using the British system, Sungusungu is divided into village chapters governed at the following levels: village, ward, district, and region but depend on the chief, ntemi, as a religious diviner to control its effectiveness (Bukurura, 1994; Abrahams, 1998). The chairman gives order in meetings while the secretary records attendance and case details discussed during court and meeting sessions.

Sungusungu are generally peacemakers, although they later received a negative reputation over the years for killing witches, who were often elderly women suspected of being witches (Mesaki, 1995).

This chapter has given you a glimpse into the Sukuma and how their economy flourished before foreign contact. This overview shows the unique features that define the Sukuma, and although I didn't cover every area such as clothing, concepts of beauty, and how young men and women choose a life partner, the few examples I gave are representative of various features unique to the Sukuma. This brief presentation also allows you to see a possible divide that may arise when an educated Sukuma starts to compare his or her traditional values with Western ideals. Being a Sukuma, I know first-hand what it means to be educated using ideas and concepts foreign to my upbringing. At the same time, I know what it means to know aspects of my culture and to honor the logic and perspective that led our ancestors to revere such practices. One idea shared previously is the greetings whereby those involved get to share whose lineage they are associated with, and in doing so, I can testify that I have been able to identify relatives even when I am in a foreign land by simply asking the question "who is your father" or in whose name should I greet you?

Furthermore, as explained, the Sukumas are very generous, and without understanding their large family sizes, an outsider is likely to wonder why, including myself, when making a meal, we tend to cook a lot. The reason lies in the fact that we are used to cooking a lot because we grew up in large families, and thus are used to making big meals. The other reason is the interconnectedness between community members. When one family cooks, a neighbor will likely pass by. Anyone who comes to our house and finds us eating is welcome to join us, as is our custom. Keeping this in mind, even in America, I find myself making some extra food just in case someone stops by. An outsider may find it irrelevant to see a large meal when there are only four of us in the family and can criticize us for not being frugal or not mindful of the amount of food we make, while on the other we wonder why someone makes so little food when they have enough to ensure everyone is satisfied, after all, you can eat leftovers later.

Also, singing and dancing are critical aspects of our Sukuma culture, which is why I love singing and dancing. In fact, my father always sang at home, and I grew up singing in one of the choirs in our hometown. I love dancing. When music is playing, my boys hear me complaining to them, saying, "Why are you not dancing?" My mama used to dance a lot, and I can remember her dancing even when she was cooking. She would stand up, hold her "*ndinho*," spatula, and turn around elegantly to the sound of the music and then go back to her cooking with a smile and tell me, "Dance." When I remember the dancing in my village and the beautiful aspects of my own culture, I hear my mama saying dance. There are so many reasons to dance. Africa has so much to offer to itself and the world. The intercultural exchange between the Danish people and the Sukuma is a beautiful way for the Sukuma, and my fellow Africans in general, to embrace our uniqueness, knowing it is beautiful. In the poem below, listen to the sounds of my mind reflecting on why Africa should dance. This poem illustrates the pride and love I have for my culture and Africa as my home.

Mama Said Dance

Though you hear the voices of the rich tormenting your poor soul
Just dance, mama said dance, for Africa is ever strong and beautiful
Though you see the faces of civilization taken from your own land
Just dance, mama said dance, for Africa is ever strong and beautiful
Though you feel the strength of the world channeled
through your own people
Just dance, mama said dance, for Africa is ever strong and beautiful

Though you taste the sweetness
of your food shipped across the nations
Just dance, mama said dance, for Africa is ever strong and beautiful
Just dance, dance, dance, and again mama said dance,
For the highest mountain is found in Africa
Mama said dance
For the many tongues dwelling in Africa
Mama said dance
For the rarest mineral is found in Africa
Mama said dance
For the various kinds of flowers shining in Africa
Mama said dance
For the first man to inhabit the earth was found in Africa
Mama said dance
Dance so hard with the SHOUT, STRENGTH, MAJESTY,
BOLDNESS, PASSION, ZEAL,
And the LOVE Africa brings to this world
Mama said dance so hard until the world hears
the HEARTBEAT of Africa
Mama said dance, for Africa is ***ALIVE***.

Discussion Questions

1. What are the special features of your culture?

    _____

    _____

2. What cultural aspects are contradictory to your values?
    (Example: for a Sukuma, it is offensive to look someone
    straight in their eyes while in the USA, this is encouraged)

    _____

    _____

3. What do you like about your culture and what don't you like and why?

_____

_____

Research Project

Learn about the Acholi of Uganda. Conduct research about who they are, their location, population, cultural features, and interesting facts about them. The information about the Sukuma is helpful in thinking about what you could research about the Acholi people group.

Supplemental Resources
Prominent Religious Singing Groups of the Wasukuma

- Mwanza town Choir
- AIC Makongoro Choir
- AIC Shinyanga Choir
- AIC Dar es Salaam Chang'ombe Choir
- Neema Gospel Choir
- AIC Chang'ombe (CVC)
- AIC Nyakato Choir

Various Dance Groups of the Wasukuma

- Tanzania Sukuma, Bachonga Magembe
- Tanzania Sukuma Jeshi Dance
- Bagika and Bagalu
- Maganigani
- Sogota
- Wigashe

Sample Dancing Performance from Danish-Sukuma Cultural Exchange

- Danish groups
- The Utamaduni ("Culture") group,
- Watoto na Wengine ("Children and Others")
- Ikumbo ("Whip")
- Kisiwani ("Of the Island")
- Eliza Workshop
- Ung'wana Undololo Uyu

PART III

IDENTITY

CHAPTER 5

TANGLED WEB OF AFRICA'S IDENTITY

*"We reveal who we are through every choice we make;
and with every choice we make, we reshape our identities."*
BY SARTRE

IN THIS CHAPTER, I explore the concept of identity by examining the meaning, development, manifestation, and interaction between identity and social-economic matters, particularly poverty. In doing so, I seek to make a connection between culture and identity, thereby giving ideas on ways in which the two concepts cannot be separated if one is to understand why we behave in a certain way, and more importantly, why and how our cultural environment permeate and shape many aspects of our lives to the point that we articulate and answer the question "who am I" or "who are you" in ways that are shaped by our culture. Furthermore, in presenting how we perceive ourselves, we get so engrossed with our way of thinking and living in this world to the point that we forget others don't share our perspective. We forget that not everyone values our identity, which, in turn, leads us to desire to convince others that our identity needs to be respected. In doing so, we ignore that valuing diversity comes after one understands and accepts that it is okay to have multiple ways of living in this world.

Drawing from Okot pBitek's chapter, *"Indigenous social ills,"* and his popular poem titled *"Song of Lawino and Song of Ocol,"* readers get to see ways in which ideas of modern and traditional values can be a cause of contention, especially for Africans who have been raised in Africa and later gain a European or Western perspective. Such identity struggle is well illustrated through the story of Phiona Mutesi, a champion Chess player from Uganda whose life is shown through the movie *Queen of Katwe*. You will gain an appreciation of the identity clash that many Africans go through. You will be able to critically examine social and cultural aspects of people who experience extreme poverty and what happens when they get a chance to be educated and taste some of the social and economic benefits of receiving formal education and the opportunity to better their lives economically. The chapter concludes with a welcome to examine how formal education and opportunities to advance socially and economically have affected how we look at those without such opportunities. More importantly, the chapter guides us to ask tough questions about our sense of identity.

Meaning and Categories of Identity

In chapters three and four, we explored the concept of culture, learned it's complicated meanings, and read a glimpse of the Sukuma people and aspects that mark their culture. Let us first remember that culture is essentially the constant negotiation of values, beliefs, behaviors, and attitudes that are patterned and learned. Therefore, culture shapes many aspects of our lives, including what we believe to be true or false, what we regard to be right and wrong, and even what we end up liking and hating, even more, the habits we consciously and unconsciously display. These cultural influences form our identities. Identity can be defined in so many ways to the point that scholars suggest "it is time to let go of the concept of identity altogether and to move beyond a scholarly language that . . . is hopelessly vague and has obscured more than it has revealed. Even we must concede that the current state of the field amounts to definitional anarchy" (Abdelal, Herrera, Johnston & McDermot (2006, p.696). A widely used concept of identity was developed by Erikson (1951, 1968) through the lens of commitment and discovery; the term was later used similarly with the idea of self-concept. Other scholars believe identity is a way in which a person makes sense of some facet or element of self-concept (Abrams, 1999; Hogg, 2003; Tajfel & Turner, 2004).

For the sake of our discussion, identity is what a person thinks about himself or herself and how others say he or she is. In the dictionary, identity is "the fact of being who or what a person or thing is" or, according to Wikipedia, "Identity is the qualities, beliefs, personality, looks and/or expressions that make a person or group." Therefore, identity is a concept that encompasses both personal and collective attributes. Thus, some scholars define this idea from a plural and dynamic perspective. Leary and Tangney (2012) suggest,

> "Identities are the traits and characteristics, social relations, roles, and social group memberships that define who one is. Identities can be focused on the past-what used to be true of one, the present-what is true of one now, or the future-the person one expects or wishes to become, the person one feels obligated to try to become, or the person

one fears one may become. Identities are orienting, they provide a meaning-making lens and focus one's attention on some but not other features of the immediate context" (p. 69).

Our identities are a critical part of self-perception and can be divided into various categories. However, I focus on three namely, personal, social, and cultural identities. Some scholars argue that categorizing certain identity features as 'personal' and others as 'social' does not seem reasonable by analyzing identity content, which, according to William James' (1892),

> "In its widest possible sense, [. . .] a man's *Me* is the sum total of all that he CAN call his, not only his body and his psychic powers, but his clothes and his house, his wife and children, his ancestors and friends, his reputation and works, his lands and horses, and yacht and bank account. All these things give him the same emotions. If they wax and prosper, he feels triumphant; if they dwindle and die away, he feels cast down—not necessarily in the same degree for each thing, but in much the same way for all" (p. 177).

However, one might argue for a distinction between personal and social identity processes. In this view, social identity is 'social' because it takes place and makes sense within social exchanges occurring among people and is externally organized through membership Rather than 'personal,' internally within a person's mind (Smith, 2011; Rattansi & Phoenix, 2005). Even more importantly, we can look at identities as inevitably both personal and social in their content, as well as in the processes that create, maintain, and change them. Nevertheless, we must understand what personal and social identity mean and how they differ even if we believe they can or cannot be separated. Personal identities consist of self-elements that are mostly private and intertwined with our life experiences. They express who we are. For example, you may identify yourself as a gardener or a country music lover. Thus, personal identity is likely to change based on a person's exposure to new experiences or when he or she encounters and develops new interests (Spreckels & Kotthoff, 2009). On the other hand, our social identities are self-elements that stem from our participation in interactive social groups we are devoted to. They align us with groups, thus allowing us to declare who we are and who we are not (Shipman, 2007; Allen, 2011).

Cultural identities are socially created classes entrenched in historical roots; they shape how we behave in this world since birth based on expectations placed on us within our societies (Yep, 2002). How we behave within public spaces may change based on various forces within our contexts and cause our cultural identity to somewhat change its image over time (Collier, 1996). Communication is one of the major ways cultural identities are expressed. Thus, learning to use members' codes is a critical step to ensure a person is acculturated and is accepted in his or her cultural group. According to Martin and Nakayama (2010), identities can be ascribed, meaning people place on us. On the other hand, they can be avowed, we assert for ourselves.

Examples of the Three Categories of Identity

Personal	Social	Cultural
Singer	Middle School Music Teacher	Chinese American
Runner	Sorority Member	Multiracial
Antique Collector	Member of Historical Society	Greek American
Comic Book Collector	Book Club Member	Gay/Lesbian
Recycler	Environmentalist	African American
Dog Lover	Member of the Humane Society	Male/Female
Teacher	Member of a Literature Club	Chaga
Chaplain	Southern Baptist Member	Sukuma
Dancer	Georgia Tech Student	Kamba

Although we can ascribe some of our identities, some characteristics are fundamentally permanent; however, depending on the context and their salient nature, the extent to which we are cognizant of them, as well as our affirmation of them, changes. For example, when my student Tatiana, who is an African American, visited Tanzania during a study abroad program, her new African friends ascribed her identity as American instead of African American. Therefore, for the Africans, their visitor's identity as American was more salient than her identity as someone of African descent. Other identities can change. For example, Yep (2002) notes that a person may change and choose certain identities over others over time; as such, one scholar described himself as an "Asian Latin American" because, during his youth, he lived in Peru and identified himself as Latina, but later started to learn about his Chinese roots which led him to accept his Chinese identity. During his college years, he embraced the American way of life. Personally, I became more aware of my African identity when I came for further studies in America, although I have been African all my life. Another friend of mine also told me that he became more aware of her American identity when he went to study abroad in Germany. So, what leads people to sometimes choose and pick, or even change, which identity they embrace at a particular stage of their lives? The answer is not straightforward, but an examination of identity development may show how, historically, dominant and nondominant identities have been formed, which in turn, may shed some light on the question at hand. In fact, such exploration may help us understand how some Africans came to embrace a western identity over their African-born identity.

Identity Development

I must make it clear that people often have many identities, and some of them overlap. Considering various forms of identity development,

I focus on the similar and different stages between how dominant and nondominant identities are established. Over the years, at a societal level, dominant and nondominant groups have been created due to some having more cultural and social recourses that enable them to have influences than other groups (Allen, 2011). Generally, the difference between dominant groups—those with more resources and influences against those with less, has been entrenched in our societies based on cultural groups. As a result, there is an uneven distribution of resources and power whereby members of dominant groups are privileged, but nondominant groups find themselves deprived. Such distinction is the foundation of various forms of institutionalized discrimination, such as sexism, racism, ableism, and heterosexism. Please note that no one is completely disadvantaged or completely privileged, just like no two people are entirely similar or entirely different. We now turn to how identity is developed.

Dominant Identity Development

According to Martin and Nakayama (2010), there are five stages involved in the development of dominant identity. First, unexamined stage—individuals in this phase do not think about their or others' identities. They are not aware of the hierarchy causing others to be treated differently, or they believe that they are not part of that system. For example, they may not see a different treatment between gender or race. If a male is paid more than a female, he may not be aware that the amount of his salary is tied to his gender. Both dominant and nondominant groups go through this stage. However, those in the dominant identity group often stay in this stage longer than the other group, who often face bias and unfairness.

Second, the acceptance stage – This has two levels, passive and active. Individuals in the passive acceptance stage acknowledge the differences in ways other people are treated but do absolutely nothing externally or internally to address it. Before you condemn and even blame those within a dominant identity for somewhat ignoring or not doing anything about this matter, please remember that the institutions I presented in chapter 3, such as family, education, religion, etc. contribute greatly to making oppression to those within the nondominant group seem normal. People in this stage would say sentences like this: "I was raised to see and treat everyone as equal; I believe we are all the same because we are all human." Although this seems wonderful, seeing everyone as equal does not mean we are equal and does not make others in the world treat everyone equally. It is at this stage people think or even insist that minorities whine. They need to work harder because they amplify their struggles. Such people do not see that institutions perpetuate certain privileges to dominant groups. Others in the acceptance stage move from being passive to becoming active. This is where such people recognize discrimination and are delighted to be in the "superior" group; unless they have frequent encounters with people from the nondominant group or become friends with one or many of them, or take a class on other cultures, they often stay at this stage and never change.

Third, the resistance stage – individuals at this phase recognize the undeserved advantages they receive. Some even feel guilty about it and want to return or disown it. After coming to this realization, they tend to avoid interaction and disconnect with their dominant group members; they retreat to the nondominant group (such as people of color), assuming they will be accepted as allies. This is a mark of improvement; however, it doesn't really address injustice. Moving to stage four, the redefining stage, means acting based on their awareness. Individuals at this stage recognize their privilege and use their roles and power to fight for social justice. For example, if they learn about identity matters or culture, they may share information with others in the same dominant class. For example, they can claim to be white or heterosexual and take action accordingly. They could say something like this: "I wish to contribute positively to this discussion, I don't want to sustain sexism, I acknowledge my maleness and talk to other men about the privileges I receive just by being male (Jones, 2009). By doing so, they counter the norms perpetuated in their societies. Stage five, which is last in the formation of dominant identity is integration. This is when people go beyond doing one thing about their dominant identity; they find opportunities and other avenues to learn, talk about and educate others about their privilege while finding ways to be allies of people in the nondominant group. They could decide to become members of an organization that allows them to be around people of the nondominant group.

Nondominant Identity Development

The nondominant identity development involves four stages, namely, unexamined, conformity, resistance, and integration (Martin & Nakayama, 2010). In the first stage, people are not aware or not interested in their own identity. For example, a young African American woman may wonder about the value of what she is being taught in February, during Black History month; she may even ask her teacher or parents to explain the reason behind learning such content. When there is great interest in a dominant group's identity, that is, when people desire to replace their own identity, they move to stage two: conformity. Here, to make people think they are different, they embrace the values and norms of the dominant culture in different ways. Some may change their name, how they look, their behavior or even the way they talk or stop using their language. For example, an African from Tanzania may try to talk through his or her nose to sound "American." I have also known friends who change their names to English names to avoid people noticing that they are likely not originally from the USA. Jones (2009) also attests that a Chicano man Moises changed his name to Moses because it was easier for his classmates to pronounce it, but he mainly made the change because it sounded "Mexican," and, upon noticing how other "brown kids" were treated by his teachers, he started identifying himself as white rather than Chicano or Mexican American. When a lesbian or gay person tries to "act straight," he is showing marks of the conformity identity development stage.

Upon realizing, despite their efforts to conform, they are still identified as different by and not counted as belonging in the dominant group, some enter the third stage: resistance and separation. Here, people in the nondominant identity group begin to confront the dominant identity group by interacting with others who share their nondominant identity. For example, a person of color who made efforts to distance himself from other minority groups may begin to interact and associate with other people of color after experiencing prejudice from white people. Likewise, a deaf person may interact more with other hearing-impaired people after being discriminated from hearing people (Allen, 2011).

When people from nondominant identity groups find a balance between accepting their own identities while appreciating other dominant and nondominant identities, they enter the integration stage. Many work hard to end discrimination even though some residual anger may remain from previous bias. Actions such as advocating for and educating others in their nondominant group as well as those in the dominant group to understand and cherish their varied identities mark the entry to this last stage of identity development in the nondominant group.

Manifestations of Identity Development among Africans

The four stages of nondominant identity development explain how Africans who grew up knowing and embracing their own culture and later found themselves embracing a western culture at some point in their lives. Here, I use an example of a well-known scholar in the field of African literature, Okot p'Bitek, to demonstrate possible stages of development among elite Africans who went through the Western education system. Please understand that this is an example; no research has been done to substantiate that he went through these stages at the times I propose here. However, looking at his writing, his perspective about his own identity can be well discerned. Additionally, no one can locate and give a specific timeframe showing a start and finish illustrative of when such stages happen in an individual. However, the tangible artifacts and behaviors of a person serve as evidence to the existence of such stages, whether they likely happened at a projected time.

Okot p'Bitek, one of Africa's prominent poets, was born in 1931 in Northern Uganda, Gulu, from a marriage between Jebedayo Opi and Lacwaa Cerina (Gauvin, 2013). Okot must have gotten his poetic roots from his mother, who was a traditional singer, storyteller, and dancer. He was from the Acholi ethnic group and hence spoke the Acholi language, a dialect prominent in Southern Luo (Al-Sharif, 2010). Okot went to Gulu high school. During these years, he was a singer, played drums and was a great soccer player. I believe Okot's life from birth to his high school age reflects the first stage of nondominant identity group—unexamined. It is evident from his interest in singing and playing the drum that he may not even have been aware of the implication of being an African. Even more, he may not have had reasons to think deeply about who he is, perhaps because he had not yet encountered circumstances that compelled him to do so.

Later, Okot attended King's College Budo, one of the oldest schools in Uganda, which was established in 1906 by the Church Missionary Society (CMS) with an intention to educate only sons of chiefs and kings (McGreggor, 2006). It was built on the land that the Kabaka (king) of Buganda donated. Later, it was owned by the Anglican Church of Uganda and became a government boarding school for boys and girls. It is highly probable that Okot became a Christian during his years at this school, thus experiencing the conformity stage of the nondominant identity group. Furthermore, at this stage, a distaste of various aspects of his African way of life is well expressed through one of his epic poems: *Song of Lawino*, a narrative in which Lawino's husband, Ocol, the son of the Acholi tribal leader, takes an educated wife, Clementine (nickname-Tina) who embraces European values and acts that way. In this poem, Ocol, who is also educated, favors Clementine and conveys his attraction to the European colonialists' culture. Lawino, a traditional African wife, demonstrates ways in which her husband shuns her. She notes:

> Husband, now you despise me
> Now you treat me with spite
> And say I have inherited the stupidity of my aunt.
> Son of the Chief,
> Now you compare me
> With the rubbish in the rubbish pit,
> You say you no longer want me
> Because I am like the things left behind
> In the deserted homestead.
> You insult me
> You laugh at me
> You say I do not know the letter A
> because I have not gone to school
> And I have not been baptized" (p'Bitek, 2013, p. 34).

In the above example, Okot, through his character Lawino shows how he feels about African culture—it is backward. He jabs at Lawino's illiteracy; not knowing "the letter A" and later adds more insults, Lawino states, "He says I am rubbish, . . . he says I am primitive . . . , he says my eyes are dead, and I cannot read, he says my ears are blocked and cannot hear a single foreign word, that I cannot count the coins" (p'Bitek, 2013, p. 35). Also, Lawino, who is the writer's tool in expressing her concern, complains about Ocol no longer being involved in her life. He has no interest in the ritualistic African dance; instead, he prefers the European-type of dance, ballroom-style. She explains, "Ocol says he does not love me anymore."

Because I cannot play the guitar and I do not like their stupid dance. Because I despise the songs they play at the ballroom dances, and I do not follow the steps of foreign songs on the gramophone records. And I cannot tune the radio because I do not hear Swahili or Luganda (p'Bitek, 2013, p. 49).

What disturbs Lawino the most is Ocol's loss of culture, and she tries her best to appeal to him to embrace his traditions and stop longing to be white. Lawino attempts to bring some sense to Ocol by showing the validity of his African culture. She explains:

Like beggars,
You take up white men's adornments
Like slaves or war captives, you take up white men's ways.
Didn't the Acholi have adornments?
Didn't black people have their ways?
Like drunken men, you stagger to white men's amusements.
Is *lawala* not a game?
Is *cooro* not a game?
Didn't your people have amusements?
Like halfwits, you turn to white men's dances,
You turn to musical instruments of foreigners (p'Bitek, 2013. P. 49)

Even more, as typical of the conformity stage in the nondominant identity development, there is a sense of wanting to change a person's appearance to look like those in the dominant identity group. In the following example, Lawino expresses Ocol's distaste for African beauty and looks down on natural hair and the natural beauty products that traditional Africans use to keep their hair and skin healthy and strong. She observes, "My husband tells me I have no ideas of modern beauty. He says I have stuck to old-fashioned hairstyles. He says I am stupid and very backward, that my hairstyle makes him sick because I am dirty" (p'Bitek, 2013, p. 50). Lawino continues to express her husband's disdain for African beauty, stating, "Ocol tells me that I like dirt. He says shea butter causes skin diseases. He says Acoli adornments are old-fashioned and unhealthy. He says I soil his white shirt if I touch him. My husband treats me as if I am suffering from the 'don't touch me' disease! He says I make his bedsheets dirty and his bed smelly. Ocol says I look extremely ugly when I am fully adorned for the dance" (p'Bitek, 2013, p. 53). These and many more examples show ways in which many Africans may display the conformity stage in the nondominant identity development journey by looking down upon their African-ness or anything originally from Africa.

For further studies, Okot went to the University of Bristol, studied law in Aberystwyth at the University of Wales. Later, he majored in social anthropology at the University of Oxford and wrote his dissertation on Lango and Acholi cultures (Gauvin, 2013). It is during this time he may have entered the third stage: resistance and separation. He once again reflects such a stage through his writing by romanticizing all that is black. He uses the same character, Lawino, who bemoans her husband's lack of African pride, and through her, expresses pride in his African culture by letting her carry a conversation with him. Lawino shows why she is proud of her African culture and expresses reasons for not liking various aspects of the European way of life. For example, Okot admits that cooking African food, such as beef or chicken, is hard because you use charcoal or firewood stove, which results in those cooking the food getting dirty during the cooking process; additionally, the food takes longer to cook because it is fresh, not frozen, but it is healthy and tastes great. On the other hand, a European stove is different—the food is frozen and does not taste as good. He writes,

> The white man's stoves are good for cooking white man's food.
> For cooking tasteless, bloodless meat of cows.
> That were killed many years ago and left in the ice to rot!
> For frying an egg which when ready is slimy like mucus,
> For boiling hairy chicken in saltless water. You think you
> are chewing paper! And the bones of the leg contain only
> clotted blood and when you bite, it makes no crackling
> sound. It tastes like earth! (p'Bitek, 2013, p. 58).

Okot is displaying what he dislikes about the other culture, thus, separating himself from "them." Although it may seem like a simple expression of a person's opinion regarding African food, which is mostly fresh because refrigeration is not available in most parts of Africa, however, rather than praising the European's stove as being sophisticated and easy to use or the Westerners' ability to preserve food for longer periods through refrigeration; instead, he focuses on what is positive about what his Africa offers. Furthermore, he starts questioning aspects of Western culture, such as "time," in ways that highlight the different worldviews. For example, Lawino shows her frustration with her husband because he is controlled by "time," and even more, he seems to lack balance between reading and enjoying his family. Lawino explains:

> My husband says I am useless because I waste time. He
> quarrels because he says I am never punctual. He says he has
> no time to waste. He tells me time is money. Ocol does not
> chat with me. He never jokes with no body. He says he has
> no time to sit around the evening fire. When my husband is

reading a new book or when he is sitting in his sofa . . . he is so silent. If a child cries or has a cough, Ocol storms like a buffalo, he throws things at the child. He says he does not want to hear noises. That children's cries and coughs disturb him! Is this not the talk of a witch? What music is sweeter than the cries of children? (p'Bitek, 2013, p. 69).

Such scorn is Okot's way of expressing what he finds culturally illogical when an outsider, in this case himself, trying to make sense of the Western way of life. Perhaps one of his sharpest depictions of his resistance or separating himself from a Western way of life, which you may also call "modern," is regarding dishes. He draws a sharp contrast between traditional African dishes and modern ones; he reveals his partiality to traditional African dishes based on their effectiveness to keep food warm. Through Lawino's voice, he notes:

In my mother's house there are no plates. We use the half gourd and the earthen dishes. The white man's plates look beautiful, but you put millet bread in it and cover it up for a few minutes, the plate is sweating and soon the bottom of the bread is wet and the whole loaf cold. A loaf in a half-gourd returns its heat and does not become wet in the bottom. And the earthen dish keeps the gravy hot and the meat steaming; and when your husband returns from a hunt or from a long day's journey, give him porridge in a half-gourd (p'Bitek, 2013, p. 61).

For the Africans who attended formal education, the ability to own fancy dishes is among the marks of climbing the social status ladder. In fact, a person able to buy "nice" dishes and eat with a fork, knife, and spoon, demonstrates his or her understanding of a Western lifestyle which includes one's ability to afford and use such dishes accordingly. Okot is illustrating the superiority of the traditional dishes, in this case "half-gourd," not due to the way it is made or its monetary value but rather, what it is able to do—keep food warm. Such expression illustrates his awareness of the value of what he has and the resources inherently present in Africa instead of focusing on "how things made in Africa by Africans" look. In doing so, he is essentially resisting the "white man's plates," thus demonstrating characteristics of being in the third level of the identity development stage. Furthermore, he commends African traditional medicine that Africans have used for decades. Through Lawino, Okot shows a variety of indigenous African plants used to cure different diseases.

> When my child is ill, I try the various Acoli herbs, I try the medicines my mother showed me. The roots of *bomo* for stomach aches; it kills poisons as well as worms. The roots of *omwombye* are chewed for bad throats, a drop in the eye kills the pains and remove the evil eye's sting. When the eyes are bursting with pain, put some *akeyo* in a pot. Cook it for some time, then expose the eyes to the steam from the pot; this burns up the spears that were in the eye. The roots of *lapena* for coughs and sore throat—you put some salt in it and chew it! The roots of *lapena* and *olim* are chewed when they have removed the blockage in the throat (p'Bitek, 2013, p.96)

Such examples are a testament that Africans have had to use their resources for a long time to fight various diseases, such as highlighted above. When Okot names one plant after another and explains what it cures, he is essentially interacting with other Africans who share a common nondominant identity. By doing so, he is allying himself with his nondominant identity group by verifying and uplifting them in a unique way.

To enter the last stage of nondominant identity development, integration, a person can show evidence of finding a sense of balance between accepting his own identity while appreciating other dominant and nondominant identities, though some anger may still linger. Here, evidence of works to advocate for and educate others within both groups becomes a clear mark of a person in the integration stage. Since Song of Lawino presents a major conflict between cultures of the nonliterate Africans who hold to their traditions, Okot, through the voice of Lawino, who symbolizes a reflection of typical East African women, showed his admiration and appreciation of his African roots as discussed above. However, in *Song of Ocol*, Okot offers a husband's response through the voice of "Ocol" to justify his cultural apostasy; he shows the strange ways of educated African elites whose new lifestyle and perspective are irreconcilable with traditional African concepts of manhood and practices acceptable and respectable in African societies. By expressing his positive view of the African culture through Lawino, and his positive opinion of western education and lifestyle through Ocol, Okot is showing a sense of balance between the two identities.

Furthermore, Okot's decision to write *Song of Lawino* initially in one of the Luo dialects in northern Uganda, Acholi, and then translate it to English shows his advocacy measures. He reached his fellow Acholi people first with a message that called them to see the value of their African traditions. In the same book, he gives examples of various African customs and values that need to be cherished as well. Even more, when he became director of Uganda's National Theatre and National Cultural Centre (1966–68), he taught his fellow Ugandans and other Africans the value of their own culture through art. In "Song of Ocol," Okot shows his fellow Africans what to value about western education, although it is different from what they know and cherish. When he lectured at various universities in Kenya and abroad, he used his western education to reach the world with his understanding of the value of his culture while acknowledging and using western education to reach them. His ability to identify the advantages of clinging to either traditional African ways of living or embracing a modern lifestyle embodies a perspective that some Africans have also embraced. Through *Song of Lawino and Song of Ocol*, Okot advocates for the African culture that has been somewhat abandoned by the educated elite, while illustrating ways in which western education has improved his social and economic status, thus showing strong evidence of reaching integration, the last stage of nondominant identity development.

It is important to acknowledge that reaching an integration stage does not mean attaining a perspective that allows someone to embrace every aspect of their new understanding of their identity. As such, Okot's ability to identify what he gained from western education, such as getting a well-paying job that enabled him to build a nice house and escape poverty, does not mean a total embrace of European ideologies and way of life. In fact, according to George Heron (1976), western education might have been a reason for Okot's decision to abandon his Christian faith to become an atheist. The intricacies of balancing between values that an African is taught to cherish while allowing herself to grow through various pathways, including western education, continues to cause a great dilemma.

Poverty and African Identity

It is one thing to know you are poor, and completely another to believe you will always be poor, regardless of how you define poverty. Even more, when you have no way of knowing you can escape poverty just because you have limited opportunities due to factors out of your control, how you feel about yourself becomes rather cumbersome. For many Africans, poverty is connected to many difficult to isolate issues. When a family struggles to make ends meet, meaning putting food on the table and hardly knowing where their next meal will come from, we call that poverty. When a mother wishes to send her children to school but cannot afford to buy school uniforms, we call that poverty. But what do you think about an African child who is born and at age three, her father dies of AIDS, leaving an African woman with no formal education to raise the children single-handedly? How would an African child like that grow up to love and cherish where she comes from only to learn she is missing so much just because her family could not afford to send her to school? And what if later she gets an opportunity to learn a game through a Christian outreach ministry that ultimately changes her life and that of her family? What about other Africans such as Mr. Robert Katende, who also face adversities in life but decide to make a difference anyway? The story of Phiona Mutesi, coupled with the role played by Mr. Katende, sheds light on ways in which traditional African values, when coupled with family and economic challenges, play a great role in shaping one's sense of identity.

Phiona was born in 1996 in East Africa, Uganda. She was born in Kampala, home of 57 slums, and grew up in Katwe, the largest of the eight slums found there (Richmond, Myers & Namuli, 2018). People resided in Katwe since the early 1970s; years of civil war resulted in its economic insecurity and led to unbelievable poverty to the point that sewage ran through the streets. Phiona's father died of AIDS when she was about three years old. She is believed to have had a sister, Julia, who also passed away with unknown causes. Her mother, Harriet Nakku, was left to care for her family as a single mother. Since she was uneducated, selling maize (also known as corn) was her only source of income to support her family. Having inherited debts that needed to be paid, a small income from her corn-selling business trapped her in a cycle of poverty and led her children, Phiona and her brother, to drop out of school. Since her mother, Harriet, cannot afford the school fees to send her to school,

Phiona is not educated and only knows the slum life. Throughout her childhood, she got severely ill and almost died twice but was able to recover. Therefore, Phiona became an aggressive child due to needing to survive in the slum.

In Katwe, a sports outreach ministry was run by an American organization founded by Russ Carr, an American man who overcame personal challenges through religion and sports. This ministry sought to offer support and religious guidance to children who live in the slums of Uganda. Rodney Suddith, another American man, took over this outreach after Carr became too old. Suddith, through his own personal experience, believes in the combination of sports and ministry to overcome challenges. When Suddith was still in charge, Mr. Robert Katende, an African man who also grew up very poor after losing his mother to AIDS at an early age, became a part of this outreach ministry. Katende was offered a soccer scholarship to fund his education up to the university level. He was injured playing soccer and almost lost his life; he later became a born-again Christian. Believing in the power of sports and religion, after university, Katende joined this sports ministry.

Several of the Ugandan children attending that ministry played soccer, but some refused, fearing they would get injured. Drawing from his experience playing chess during his university years, Katende started teaching them chess. To attract children from the Katwe slum, Katende offered a daily meal of porridge and taught them spiritual lessons. Phiona's brother discovered the ministry after word spread about the porridge provision, he decided to join the chess club. All along, life at home for Phiona continued to be challenging; Harriet offered them just one meal a day, the opportunity to get some porridge was not easy to pass. Later, Phiona follows his brother and decides to join the Chess club as well.

A few months after Phiona joined the chess project, Sports Outreach partnered with the Andrew Popp Memorial Foundation to sponsor many Ugandan children to attend school. This is how Phiona could finally go to school. Katende continued to teach the children chess and exposed them to various tournaments. After a short time, Phiona became the best among the group and won the "Under-20" national championship. After realizing her potential, Katende trained her more seriously. She won the 2008 and 2009 national junior championships. For the most part, Phiona saw life in the slum as normal. She enjoyed the food that her mother cooked for her and all her siblings. She helped her mother fetch water, sweep, and mop the house floor accordingly. She wore her tattered dresses and torn Kanga and Kitenge with contentment. She would sing and dance with the other children in the streets of Katwe as if she went on planet Mars. In 2009, Phiona and two of her teammates had the opportunity to go beyond their country; they travelled to Sudan and won the Africa's International Children's Chess Tournament. For the first time, Phiona saw what life looked like outside the slums. She boarded an airplane for the first time; she tasted ice cream, ate French fries with ketchup, and swam in a swimming pool. She started seeing a life she desired; she realized what she had was not enough. Even more, she saw a possibility for a different life. She was no longer satisfied with the ragged clothes she used to wear; she was no longer interested in helping her mother with house chores. After all, how would any of those be important than resting and gathering energy to prepare for her chess competitions? In all, she saw a path to gain access to a new world and what it had to offer.

Phiona went on to qualify for the International Chess Olympiad in Russia. This is where her African identity was once again tested. She faced older and experienced players, causing her to lose many games at the Olympiad. She wondered whether she could even compete at that level; she blamed Katende for exposing her to a life that she felt unable to attain. She wondered whether she ever belonged in a higher social class considering her poverty-stricken background. Her heart became so troubled that she felt sad to know the life outside the slum. She felt sad that she might be unable to attain the new life she desired. Even more, she questioned the value of living with her mother and wished to be with Mr. Katende's family to increase her chance of winning in the next tournaments. She found herself questioning the reason for spending a few minutes washing dishes or mopping the floor rather than studying. Mr. Katende encouraged her to find a balance between helping her mother with chores and finding time to study. This defeat became her greatest teacher and motivator. Following her loss in the Olympiad, she competed at another Ugandan national tournament and won. She became a devout born-again Christian and credits her success to her faith.

Phiona's story is unique in that she mastered a game mostly played by people who are literate. Many books are written about the game, and numerous studies have been conducted to show how to master it. How can an illiterate African child understand a complicated game of chess without attending a formal education? How is it possible for a poor African child to have a mind capable of examining and reasoning out strategies to master a game to defeat even children who came from wealthy families? Is it possible for an African child to think at a level that overwhelms people with higher levels of western education? The answer is yes. When she competed with students at Queen's college in Uganda and won, she was crowned "best boy" because she won against a boy. She even asked Mr. Katende whether she won because she didn't believe she had the ability to do better than the educated ones. On the other hand, Phiona's story is like that of many African boys and girls who face many challenges from the loss of parents, poverty, sickness, and many more. Like Phiona, though hard to believe, such circumstances do not define the abilities inherently present in each one of us. To be an African is not synonymous with unintelligent. To be an African doesn't mean you are somehow less than. To be poor does not mean your mind is poor. To be African is just a manifestation of humanity lived in Africa. To be

African is to realize opportunities to make a difference in the world, just like Mr. Katende did for Phiona and many other children in Uganda and around the world.

You see, being an African simply means experiencing life in Africa. When given opportunities to gain formal education within Africa or in a foreign country, it is an opportunity to find ways to improve a way of life but not to despise the cultural norms that made you succeed in the first place. Mr. Katende saw the value of formal education as a pathway for Phiona and her family to escape poverty, but he did not see African cultural norms that encourage hard work and respecting parents and elders as less important. Katende had the ability to take a high-paying job as an engineer but chose to make a difference in the lives of children. His decision is an example hardly celebrated in the world. Some Africans who attain high social and economic status through formal education tend to look down upon where they come from. Many despise the houses, the clothing, the hair, the language, and even the food they grew up eating, to name just a few. Once they taste another life outside of their hometowns and villages, everything once adorable and admirable becomes something to be ashamed of rather than to be celebrated.

After Phiona won the national championship, she began teaching other children, thus drawing international publicity to herself and the chess project led by Katende. Consequently, she attended secondary school but continued to face many challenges. Her family was still in the slums; she could have ended up falling into single motherhood if she followed her elder sister Night's footsteps. She faced the cultural pressure of becoming a mother or finding a man able to support herself and her family, hence risking ending her chess career as well as her education. All these challenges are not limited to Phiona as an African; they are problems that anyone may face in any part of the world.

Poverty is not synonymous with being African. Poverty is like a problem in the world, today it may be mine, but tomorrow it may be yours. The challenge is that many Africans have fallen into believing that they cannot be more than the perceived poverty that everyone expects them to have. If we are honest, most of us have fallen into believing that we cannot be more than the world believes we can be. Most of us hear such lies constantly to the point that we start believing in them. Well, the truth is, the only thing that separates the poor from the rich is often opportunities. Phiona's pathway to success was, for the most part, tied to the opportunity she later received. Therefore, when doors of success are hidden and sometimes intentionally shut by those able to let Africans shine, they often believe in a never-ending circle of poverty. However, when Africans look deep down within themselves and their communities, many create their own opportunities and find ways to escape poverty with or without a helping hand from a foreign country. In fact, many wealthy Africans became economically successful without a single degree, while others succeeded after receiving formal education. Therefore, identity struggles among Africans are compounded with other complex issues that, although they can be specific to Africa, are also common challenges that should go hand in hand with life circumstances that can happen to anyone.

Supplemental Resources and Ideas

- Rent or purchase the book *The Queen of Katwe* to learn more about Phiona's story.
- Conduct research on the status of women in a specific African country. For example, you may research the status of women in Uganda in politics, sports, education, and much more. You could examine where Phiona is currently and what she is doing in various aspects of her personal and professional life.
- What is your perspective about sports ministry in developing countries? Are you familiar with any other ministries such as

this in other parts of the world? If not, what type of ministries do you feel are best suited to make a difference for young people in impoverished contexts around the world?

- Watch the movie *Queen of Katwe.* https://www.youtube.com /watch?v=poEdA5WvfAw

While Watching, Answer the Following Questions

1. Where is this movie situated—name the country?

_____

_____

2. Who is Robert Katende?

_____

_____

3. What program did Robert Katende develop at a nearby mission?

_____

_____

4. Why were Phiona and her brother unable to go to school?

_____

_____

5. Why did Mr. Katende refuse to take a high-paying job as an engineer?

_____

_____

6. When Phiona lost in Moscow, what was the problem?

_____

_____

7. In your own perspective, who played a great role in Phiona's success?

_____

_____

8. What gender issues were presented in this film?

_____

_____

9. What surprised you in this film?

_____

_____

10. What is your perspective about religious-based outreach ministries?

_____

_____

11. What did you like or NOT like the most in this film?

_____

_____

12. Comment on anything you would like.

_____

_____

CHAPTER 6

CRITICAL MATTERS ON AFRICANS' IDENTITY

"Mother, why was I born black?"
(PBITEK, 2013, P.126)

IN THIS CHAPTER, I present and examine major perceptions of African identity to help us understand critical issues regarding ways in which Africans feel about themselves and how they are perceived by others around the world. Even more, drawing from historical perceptions about Africans, I examine ways in which Africans have addressed specific aspects of their identity that tend to mostly affect them in various facets of their lives within the African continent and in the diaspora: specifically, names and skin color. To illustrate the various tiers of identity and their intricate expressions, I present examples of prominent Africans within and beyond Africa, former president Baraka Obama, the late Dr. Maya Angelou, and the late

Dr. John Pombe Magufuli. Subsequently, I demonstrate how an activity such as an "identity interview" will encourage you, your family, and friends to reflect on your perceptions of identity. I also highlight a few samples of reflections done by various students after taking "the Swahili and the World II" class to show how everyone may find ways to apply ideas discussed in this book. The chapter commences with a presentation of my own reflection of identity, thus encouraging readers to take time to consider their perceptions of identity and to see how myself and many Africans revolutionize their sense of identity.

African Identity in Question

I will never forget a phrase that one of my former professors told me on the first day of her class; "Dainess, what are you doing here? none of *your kind* ever pass my class." Rather than being worried or scared of failing, I just couldn't figure out what she meant by "your kind." In fact, in any given moment, we see differences and human identity using frameworks and thus run into problems understanding each other's frame and meeting others where they are. The problem was that we each had different frameworks in our minds regarding a concept that we both thought had a common meaning. As mentioned in the previous chapter, identity is complex because it is a result of a person's family and other roots that play a major role in his/her life. Identity is related to a sense of self and its continuity over a period and location. Identity focuses on ways in which we express differences (Leary & Tangney, 2012). Based on the three categories of identity explored in the previous chapter—namely, personal, social, and cultural—I now believe there are three levels of human identity that shape how people express differences: individual, universal, and social group.

At the individual human level is a strong emphasis on aspects that differentiate one person from the other. Thus, no person is like any other. Each person has a personality, experiences, fingerprints, and many more that are unique to him or her. People who view others from this perspective tend to value aspects that make every person unique; they often resist putting people into groups; they are against notions that use a broad brush to paint a picture of a person based on others with comparable features. Such people prefer to focus on varied manifestations and pathways of living in the world. People taking this framework undermine the labels assigned to others based on social group identities. They are also likely to omit many features that many people have in common. At the universal human level is a strong emphasis on sameness. Aspects that all human beings have in common, such as needing food and water or bleeding, are mostly underscored. People who view others from this point of view prefer to focus on similar aspects that connect people. These are people who see every aspect present in people as key aspects that need to be acknowledged by minimizing features that make us different. You may find them saying things like "we all bleed the same way, or we all hurt, and we all cry" or "why don't we all live in harmony? After all, we come from the same human race, and we are cut from the same cloth of humanity." People who put emphasis on this viewpoint often tend to dismiss the differences inherently present in people; they forget the varied ways people experience life at the individual and even social level.

At the level of social group is an emphasis on specific qualities such as physical and mental ability, age, race, gender, culture, socioeconomic status, sexual orientation, to name a few, shared by a group of people, which in turn differentiate them from others. Here, people say, we are different from some people and like some others. People taking this standpoint acknowledge the varied ways we are each shaped and judged by societies, organizations, and groups in which we live. I believe the social group identity level is misunderstood the most. This is a level laden with power inequities. In the example I gave previously, my teacher had put me in a specific social group, which, according to her experiences, people with certain features happened to fail her class. I, on the other hand, didn't share her experience, nor was I raised in the same society. Thus, I didn't know which group she was assigning me. As a result, she labeled me as part of a group that I may or may not have belonged to. Did she put me in a group of Africans in general or people from my country of Tanzania, or married women getting undergraduate degrees in a foreign land, or people with short hair? The list can go on. Those taking this framework often tend to stereotype or neglect the ways in which people within groups still have different experiences and various features that tend to set them apart from most people within the same group.

Practically, however, we each use all three frames at different times and contexts. It is therefore important for us to realize and admit that all three perspectives exist. When presenting and talking about other people who are different from us, we need to recognize which framework is at work. Even more importantly, we each need to know when to emphasize our uniqueness from each other and how we fit with others in specific ways while acknowledging what brings us together as humans. When we know which level we are communicating at, and work to meet each other at that level, whether social group, universal or individual, we are likely to understand each other better and even seek to respect our varied differences. Bearing this in mind, Africans have been presented in positive and negative ways from all three levels of identity. Although people tend to use other features to put Africans in specific social groups, allow me to use names and skin color. I use these features to highlight historical and current identity issues that Africans face and address to bring a revolution to the "African-ness" as an identity label.

African Identity Labels
Names: Meaning and Naming Practices in Africa

What is in a name? I was told at a very young age that every person often has three names: the name given by parents, the name others give us (based on our reputation), and the name we give ourselves (our character). Even in the Bible, it reads, "A good name is more desirable than great riches; to be esteemed is better than silver or gold" Proverbs 22:1. Therefore, we can all agree that a name is more than a label to distinguish you from a crowd of people or one you answer to when someone calls you; a name is endowed with immeasurable value that money cannot buy. In fact, you and I have control of some aspects of our names, but we ought to know the limits of our power to control our names. Understandably, the inability for one to control the name given by parents is an incentive to examine what guides parents in Africa to name their children, the significance of knowing what lies behind each African name, and ways in which changing such names has great implications regarding identity. In doing so, you will understand that names and naming are central to creating, sustaining, and reclaiming African identity. According to Liseli Anne Maria-Teresa Fitzpatrick (2012), names are not mere elements of cultural retention. They are also a form of resistance; they play a critical role in constructing identity, especially for people of African descent. She notes,

> "European colonizers attacked and defiled African names and naming systems to suppress and erase African identity – since names not only aid in the construction of identity, but also concretize a people's collective memory by recording the circumstances of their experiences. Thus, to obliterate African collective memories and identities, the colonizers assigned new names to the Africans or even left

them nameless, as a way of subjugating and committing them to perpetual servitude" (p. ii).

To understand the significance of names among people of African descent, one must recognize the spirituality that unites African people together and shapes their physical reality. Based on the African cultural perspective, spirit is the core of everything. The *utamawazo*, Afrocentric worldview shows that African people still residing in Africa and those scattered in the diaspora experience reality as a union between both the spiritual and the material (Fitzpatrick, 2012). For Africans, a person's name has divine powers, signifying the essence of his spirit. Bernhardt (2001) notes, "When one bestows a name upon a child, that person is not simply naming the flesh of the child, but rather the name is for the person's soul" (p.7). Africans believe that everything has spirit. Thus, it is given a name; for this reason, African people name everything, including places, things, and animals (Bernhardt, 2001). The nature and time for naming practices among Africans vary across the continent. Thus, I highlight some examples of the varied naming practices to demonstrate the meaning behind a name given to an African child.

In South Africa, among the Nguni-speaking people and the Zulu, for example, "igama" is the word for name, meaning "your symbol." Fitzpatrick (2012) elaborates, "Its original meaning being a symbol engraved upon a flat stone. In some early African societies, when a child was given a name, the symbolic meaning of the child's name was painted on a round pebble in red or black pigment, and this symbol was kept for as long as the person lived. Upon death, the "named-pebble" was broken into two pieces and returned to earth's bed – transcending back into the spiritual realm" (p.26). In her book *African Names – Reclaim Your Heritage,* Sharon Bernhardt (2001) notes a similar idea, that a child's name was carved on a piece of hardwood with a sharp stone; upon the person's death, the carved wood was ceremoniously burnt in a special fire lit just for this reason. Likewise, instead of burning a symbolic object that had a person's name, other people in Africa choose to mention it seldomly in a special way. Among the Batswana and Sotho-speaking people, *Leena* is the word for name; it means staying, remaining behind, essentially meaning all that stays behind after your death. This idea signifies the immortality aspect of a person's name. A name is believed to possess immense spiritual power such that a change to a person's name would be harmful accordingly. For this reason, a person's true name was not revealed until trust was established. For example, "if your name was *Lesedi*, which in Tswana or Sotho means 'light,' and an adversary wanted to cause harm to you, all s/he needed to do was reverse your name to *Lefifi*, which means 'darkness'" (p. 27). Talking with many of my fellow African friends, I learned that in Central Africa, among the Congolese of the Kongo ethnic group, a newborn was not regarded as truly human until a name was assigned.

In West Africa, the Akan-speaking people of Ghana base their names on the day of the week because they believe that to be the day a person's soul incarnated the body. For example, a friend's name is *Kojo*; he was given that name because he is male and was born on Monday. He said that a girl born on Monday would be called *Adwoa*.

In Tanzania, East Africa, among the Sukuma people of which I belong to, names are given based on event, circumstance, or season. For example, *Sami* means one (female) who moves or relocates often, given if a child is born when the family was relocating; *Samanangu* means moving light, fast and often, given if the family moved a lot without taking most of their possessions. *Mashiku* means days or thousand. A child named *Mashiku* or *Shiku* was given this name if born around many days of sorrow. Pertaining to a name given based on circumstance, a good example is my mother-in-law, whose name was *Bageme*. Bageme's mother—Bulegani, had three daughters from another marriage with Masanja, who later passed away. After the passing of Masanja, his distant relative, Sweke, was asked to marry Bulegani to keep the family line and to provide for the three daughters. When Bulegani and Sweke got married, the people in their village wondered if their marriage would work, saying in Sukuma, *leka bageme*, let them try. Therefore, when Bulegani and Sweke had their first child, they named her *Bageme* because everyone was saying "*leka bageme*."

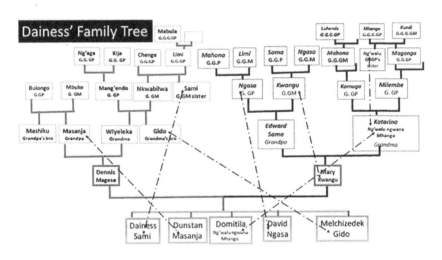

Also, the Sukuma name their children to connect them to their ancestral lineage. Thus, children may be named after a parent or a grandparent. The above family tree illustrates how names are inherited throughout family lines. Starting with me, Dainess, my father is Dennis Magese, who married my mom, Mary (Kwangu) Sama. I am the firstborn of five children. Each of us has a given Christian name (on the top line) and a family given name (on the bottom line). Dainess is my given Christian name; it means a holy place. I was born when my father was a Roman Catholic and thus named me under saint Dainess. Dad doesn't really know why he liked Saint Dainess!! Sami is my family's given name, which connects me to my ancestral line. I was named after my great-grandmother's sister, Sami. My parents say, when I was born, my paternal grandmother, Wiyeleka was there. Therefore, she was given the privilege to name me. Since she was very fond of her aunt (her mother's sister) Sami, she decided to give me that name. My brother, Dunstan, was named after our paternal grandfather, Masanja. My sister Domitila was named after our maternal grandmother, Ng'walu ng'wana Mhango, abbreviated "Mhango." Likewise, my brother David was given our maternal great grandfather's name, Ngasa. My youngest brother Melchizedek was named after my paternal grandmother's brother—Gido.

When I got married to Fabian Abedinego Maganda, we were blessed with two handsome boys, Dennis Azariah and Enock Ebeneza. We named our children with two names, a Christian given name and a family given name. We named our firstborn after my father Dennis, while Enock was named after my father-in-law, Enock. Azariah is a Christian name that means God is my help. In the years leading to Dennis' pregnancy, I had several health challenges. When he was born, my husband and I named him "God is my help"-Azariah because we believed having a baby at the time was only possible through supernatural power. A year later, I conceived a second son. Considering the condition of my health, we named him Ebeneza, meaning "stone of help," to commemorate divine power and provision. Notice, the original Hebrew name is spelled with an "er" at the end; however, we spell his name "Ebeneza" with an "a" at the end to signify the Swahili phonetics, just the way the name sounds.

Like the Sukuma, the Yoruba-speaking people also give names based on events surrounding the child's birth. When a child is born, there is a sense of anticipation that her spirit will be united with her ancestors, as noted in the Oríkì, a special song recited at the naming ceremony. Carmichael explains,

> The oríkì is said publicly in the ear of the child and then to the community, to welcome the infant into world. The oríkì imprints the child with its complex historical, spiritual, and social identities . . . it is a meditation on the meaning and significance of the new human's name. It is an evocation of the strong deeds, character, and praise names of the infant's ancestors, and, perhaps most important, it is an optimistic attempt to project (and define) in ways desirable ways the child's future personality. By evoking lineage, the oríkì is ultimately about spiritual inheritance: that eternal life force that has many names (Ase among the Yoruba, Magara among the Dogon, Ike among the Igbo), which we receive from our ancestors." Ture &Thelwell (2003, p. 97).

The Oríkì is like the Izibongo, a name which a child is given among the Zulu people of South Africa, signifying not only the circumstance but also the identity of ancestors related to the child. In the end, when you know a person's name, you know their story. For that reason, the late Miriam Makeba, a famous South African singer, songwriter, and activist, tried to ensure that her African name was written correctly. Thus, she wrote a letter to the editor of the Times Magazine, saying:

> Dear Editor,
> There was a slight error, which I do not think you will mind my calling attention to. It concerns my African

name. I would like to spell it correctly for you: Zenzile Makeba Qgwashu Nguvama Yiketheli Nxgowa Bantana Balomzi Xa Ufun Ubajabulisa Ubaphekeli, Mbiza Yotshwala Sithi Xa Saku Qgiba Ukutja Sithathe Izitsha Sizi Khabe Singama Lawu Singama Qgwashu Singama Nqamla Nqamla Nqgithi.

The reason for its length is that every child takes the first name of all his male ancestors. Often following the first name is a descriptive word or two, telling about the character of the person, making a true African name somewhat like a story" (Miriam Makeba, New York City, Feb 29, 1960).

As Makeba noted, there is a story behind an African name— some more elaborate than others. Either way, a mark of history, day, circumstance, ancestry, or destiny, to name just a few, accompanies an African child. Changing a name, therefore, implies much more than just a label. It erases a major essence of an African. Bearing this in mind, I wish to give a few examples of ways in which African names were changed, sometimes voluntarily but for the most part, without choice.

Impact of Colonization and Religion on African Names

As noted previously, names and practices while naming an African child held a special meaning. When slavery, colonization, and non-African religion touched Africa, they had a great impact on African names and naming practices all over the African continent as well as throughout the African Diaspora. For one, names were no longer historical markers with story and significance but, rather, a mere label that meant nothing to the African men and women. Instead, it was an identification tool of various aspects of their new enslaved state. For example, slaves shipped to colonial masters were first branded, putting marks that identified the ship from which they were brought in and where they were taken before being shipped. Captain Thomas Phillips, an interloper during the slave trade, explains, "We mark'd the slaves [whom] we had bought on the breast or shoulder with a hot iron, having the ship's name on it, the place being before anointed with a little palm oil, which caused but little pain, the mark being usually well in four or five days" (Thomas, 1997, p. 396). Slaves were further branded to mark a sense of baptism. . . . Elaborates, "What is the very first thing—richly symbolical—that Crusoe, the enlightened eighteenth-century European, does with this cannibal, this "savage" whose life he has saved? He exercises the divine and sovereign right of christening: he names him" (McGrane, 1989, p. 48).

Hugh Thomas further shows that a cross was marked on slave's royal arms, the letters "DY" were placed on those belonging to the Royal Africa Company whose chairman was Duke of York, thus the letters "DY." Thomas (1997, p.398) continues,

> "In the early seventeenth century, it became customary for slaves in Africa to be baptized before their departure from Africa. This requirement was first laid down by King Philip III of Spain (II of Portugal) in 1607 and confirmed in 1619. The slaves had, as a rule, received no instruction whatever before this ceremony, and many, perhaps most, of them had no previous indication that there was such a thing as a Christian God. So, the christening was perfunctory. In Luanda, the captives would be taken to one of the six churches, or assembled in the main square. An official catechist, a slave, say, who spoke Kimbundu, the language of Luanda, would address the slaves on the nature

of their Christian transformation. Then a priest would pass among the bewildered ranks, giving to each one a Christian name, which had earlier been written on a piece of paper. He would also sprinkle salt on the tongues of the slaves and follow that with holy water. Finally, he might say, through an interpreter: Consider that you are now children of Christ. You are going to set off for Portuguese territory, where you will learn matters of the Faith. Never think any more of your place of origin. Do not eat dogs, nor rats, nor horses. Be content."

Once they reached ashore, in the following years, many African slaves were labeled as objects with numbers such as slave #1, slave #2 to aid with keeping track of human stock, strictly for bookkeeping, and to make it easy for the slave master to identify them; sometimes they were called "girl" or "boy." These assigned slave names later became racist insults that whites used to call African Americans, including nigger, sambo and boy' (Heller, 1975). Still in the twentieth century, in Africa, naming became a complicated reality. As Simmonds (2005) elaborates,

My paternal grandparents named me Nkweto wa Chilinda. But the name arrived too late. Time had moved on. This was the middle of the twentieth century. The modern age. Modernity had implications for my very identity in colonial central Africa, what is now Zambia. When I was born, my parents also gave me a name, as they waited for the ancestors to grant me life. This was taking time. Messages and letters took weeks to get to my grandparents' village and back. I had to be called something and my father found an English name for me from a book that he was reading. Nora. In my father's house I'm still called

Nora. In terms of names, I was born at the wrong time. The postwar colonial African society into which I was born was having a crisis of identity. A separation of the old order from the new. Families were literally torn apart, separated by the idea of progress itself. Having an English name was symbolic. It was one way that you could show you were of the modern world . . . could speak English . . ." (p.112).

In addition to the two names, Nkweto wa Chilinda and Nora, she also acquired another Christian name, Felistas; to her and many others in those days, "names symbolized another existence. A God beyond our imagination. A Christian God . . . Mary, Joseph, James . . . Felicitas" (p. 112). However, her African identity slowly started to be violated. First, she was not named according to the customs and practices of her own people. She states:

There are many things wrong with the way I was named. The first being that I shouldn't carry a name from my father's family at all. As AbaBemba we are matrilineal. The maternal spirits of the ancestors should be passed onto the child through the given name. This does not imply a female name, but a maternal ancestor, female or male. Names are not gendered. My mother's grandmother delivered me. By ancestral right she should also have named me. That was my first loss, the first confusion in my identity. I was born at a time when AbaBemba men were acquiring authority over their wives and children based on the new ways of the modern world. The right to name me was a loss for my mother and all our foremothers, and a loss for me, who carries my father's people's spirit, I who am denied a continuation of the female line (Simmonds, p. 112).

She further explains, upon joining school at the age of ten, her name was Nora Nkweto Mfula. However, she felt compelled to change her name. First, she dropped the name "Nkweto" completely because it was regarded as a pagan name. Furthermore, Nora, though an English name, was not good enough. In a Catholic school, she was supposed to take a name of a saint because "the saint was your guardian, could mediate on your behalf—a shortcut to God, or even better still to the Virgin Mary . . ." (p. 113). In her school, they were to use Western names. African names were to be used only as "surnames" in order to avoid being confused with "white" children. She decided to name herself Felistas, in short, Felly. Later in life, she encountered another name, Simmonds. Thus, in her driving license, her full name reads Felicitas Nora Nkweto Simmonds.

Like many Africans who reside in Africa and others in the diaspora, our names mean more than a label. To feel truly free, many efforts to reclaim African names have been made; a closer look at African American names reflect this reality. For example, I know many who adopted Swahili names, for example, *Nia* – a Swahili name, meaning intention, *Amani* – a Swahili name meaning peace, and many more. Other African activists have made efforts to change their names accordingly. For example, Mphande (2006) contends that "through re-naming themselves, African Americans have continued the process of cultural formulations and reclaiming of their complex African roots in the continuing process of redefining themselves and dismantling the paradigm that kept them mentally chained (p. 104). However, others such as Simmonds (2005) bring another aspect regarding the names given to Africans during and postcolonial era, and why many have chosen to keep their indigenous African names while retaining European names. She writes,

"Often, I drop Nora, it is the name I least relate to, unless I'm in Zambia, which is not often these days. I haven't been there since my mother died three years ago. Sometimes I feel that I can't go back. However, these days Nkweto is with me now in a way that I haven't felt before. It could be because of my mother's death. I need to feel close to her spirit, through my own spirit, Nkweto wa Chilinda. Recently I've used it when I write poetry, when I write from my soul, when I'm saying something that touches my very core. In public, at conferences for example, I insist that my full name appears on my name tag. In a society that cannot accommodate names that come from 'other' cultures, this can be a frustrating exercise. It is no wonder that many Black children will Anglicize their names to avoid playground taunts . . . and much worse. We are still fighting colonialism. Friends ask me why I don't just drop my non-African names. It would be a good idea, but not a practical one. In reality, my reason has nothing to do with practicality, it has to do with my own identity. For better, for worse, my names locate me in time and space. It gives me a sense of my own history that I not only share specifically with a generation of people in Africa but also with all Africans in the Diaspora (p.114).

I cannot present all there is concerning the various aspects of African names prior to and post-colonial domination. However, one point is clear, for Africans, names before foreign contact and domination were a sign and act that united the living soul with his or her ancestral spirit while emphasizing a time, event, circumstance, or season. Such significance was lost during the era of slavery and colonial rule in addition to voluntary and involuntary changes brought by religion. Upon receipt of their independence, Africans knew they needed to reclaim their names as a form of resistance. In many areas, the battle still goes on because African names, though a wonderful identity, in America, for example, are easily discernable and are thus a target of discrimination that allows some to miss a chance to be called for an interview for a job. To this date, however, many Africans continue to name their children freely and confidently, knowing the power and significance of their African roots; they continue to search and proclaim to the world the value and power of where they come from, and they know they have the right to honor their identity. As Warner-Lewis (2003) concludes, ". . . the adoption of African names can be seen '. . . either [as] an outright rejection of Eurocentricity or its converse – a positive recognition of African ethnicity'– or both" (p.80).

Skin Color

Skin color has once more become an issue at the forefront of news around the world, especially in America, considering the prominence of the Black Lives Matter movement surrounding multiple killings by the police of people of color, specifically, African Americans. How would you feel if, from a young age, you got used to hearing that you are worth less than another person mainly because you are black? You don't have to use a lot of imagination to understand that years of being told you are unworthy taints your sense of worth. For many decades back and to this date, people with lighter skin have been favored over the darker-skinned ones. In fact, the world seems to revolve around the belief that "white is right; black is bad." In fact, "in almost every Negro family, the lighter children are favored by the parents" (Grambs,1965, p. 14). People didn't just wake up one day and start making this color distinction. As history testifies, the color game that resulted in the negative perception of black people can be credited mainly to ways in which slave masters treated their slaves based on the shades of their skin. Historically, slave masters treated black people with lighter skin better. The dark-skinned blacks were put to work in the fields and were known as "field Negroes" while the ones with light skin worked in the house and were referred to as "house Negroes." Brown slaves, who were born out of slave masters taking advantage of black women slaves, were also given more respect. Subsequently, lighter-skinned blacks were respected more, not only by slave masters but also by the dark-skinned blacks. As a result, consciously and subconsciously, black people learned from watching others and without realizing it, they also taught themselves that white is better than black.

In Africa, things were not any better. In the Swahili coastal states, for example, Arabs who traded with the Swahili people for many years before enslaving them started by first marrying African concubines (Maganda, 2014; Gates, 1999). Such decisions resulted in children who were mixed blood; they had brown or lighter skin. As years went by, those Arab-African children inherited land and properties tied to their non-African fathers; as a result, they were worth more than the purely dark-skinned Africans who had little to no ownership of land, mainly because intergenerationally, they were slaves. Even when I was growing up, in the late 1960s and early 1970s; among the Sukumas, a light-skinned girl received more cows (bride-price) than a dark-skinned one because it was believed that there was white blood in her ancestry, thus, likely to have rights to a piece of land.

Nagar (2018) elaborates well on the whiteness vs. black battle even among Indians. She notes, "Internalization of superiority of fair/white skin has been related to the combined influences of colonialism, caste system, and globalization. Many South-Asian countries like India, Pakistan, Sri Lanka, Nepal, and so on were ruled by the British for around 200 years; 'white' race was the ruler, and the 'dark' native were the ruled. This led to internalization of superiority and power of the "white" skin and inferiority and powerlessness of the 'dark skin'" (p.2). To date, in many disciplines, research shows skin color bias impacts relationships and interactions between various groups of people (Gullickson, 2005; Robinson, 1992; Wade & Bielitz, 2005). For example, in the 1967 movie *Guess Who's Coming for Dinner*, skin color played a great role in the disapproval of a relationship between a white woman and a black man who found themselves in love. More specifically, a white woman, Joanna Drayton (Katharine Houghton) fell in love and became engaged to a black doctor: John Prentice (Sidney Poitier). Joanna's parents, Matt Drayton (Spencer Tracy) and his wife Christina (Katharine Hepburn), lived in San Francisco. They were very wealthy. Per usual, after the engagement, Joanna decided to take her fiancé to meet the parents. One evening, Joanna's parents decide to invite John's parents for dinner. When both sides of the couple meet, they greatly disapprove of the relationship. Skin color sometimes cannot be separated from race. As in this movie example, John's academic and professional achievement seemed insufficient and didn't matter in getting the approval to marry Joanna. I wish I could say only Joanna's parents had a problem with this relationship, but John's parents did too. When you think about it, the issue gets much more complicated. In Africa, for example, skin color and relationships are complicated to a greater degree.

In the 2008 movie *Skin*, skin color once again played a great role in complicating the relationship between Sandra Laing and a black South African man. In this film, which is based on a true story, Sandra Laing (Sophie Okonedo) looks like a light-skinned black girl, but she is the biological daughter of Alice Krige and father Sam Neill—who are both white. Sandra possesses all the characteristics present among black people, such as thick hair oh sometimes called "nappy hair." On the other hand, biologically, she belongs to a genealogy of white people who somehow ended up having a brown girl. This film is situated in the late 1950s, when South Africa was at the height of apartheid. Outwardly, Sandra is black, or you may call her brown. You may also say mixed, but she looks remarkably different from her parents. Biologically, however, she was confirmed to be the daughter of Alice Krige. Fortunately, or unfortunately, depending on how you want to look at it, Sandra falls in love with a black South African man. This is where the battle started, she feels more comfortable with her black African man, but on the other hand, her parents disapprove of the relationship. Even more, legally, she is not supposed to be in contact with black people. For her to have a relationship with the love of her life, she must be classified as black. At first, her father fought so Sandra would be classified as white even though she looked black. However, later, Sandra herself fought to be classified as black so she could be with the love of her life. Sandra leaves her parents to be with her husband's African family. You'll be better off watching the film to appreciate this struggle. Sandra is in a dilemma, is she white or black; the truth doesn't seem to matter. The world and the people around her judge her based on her skin color. To herself and everyone around her, she is black. Once again, skin color dictated all aspects of her life. It dictated her sense of identity and how she was treated by others, including her own family and that of her husband.

Unfortunately, skin color is a constant struggle all over the world. Most of us are defined by the color of our skin. If we are honest, we would realize that the people around us are likely to judge us by skin color first before they get to know us. But many times, black people face negative aspects of humanity solely based on skin color (Celious & Oyserman, 2001; Hill, 2002a). In America, for example, light-skinned people have better occupations, earn a high income, and often have more educational opportunities than those with darker skin color (Hall, 2005; Maddox & Gray, 2002). Furthermore, among black high school students, intelligence, popularity, attractiveness, to name just a few, are attributed to peers with lighter skin (Bond & Cash,1992; Stephens & Few, 2007). Even in the medical field, particularly among psychologists, skin color influences how clients are treated. For example, Atkinson, Brown, Parham, Matthews, Landrum-Brown, and Kim (1996) show white psychologists identified and ascribed more severe mental disorders for Black clients with darker skin while rating Black clients with lighter-skin simpler disorders; they marked them more attractive as well as expressing positive feelings toward them.

Also, compared to lighter-skinned blacks, Maddox and Gray (2002) show that darker-skinned Blacks are more likely to face greater barriers to achievement. Other studies show dark-skinned individuals are often seen as less attractive (Kaufman & Wiese, 2011; Watson, Thornton & Engelland, 2010), while in the justice system, people with darker skin tend to experience more racial discrimination (Klonoff & Landrine, 2000) and are given severer legal sentence (Eberhardt, Davies, Purdie-Vaughns, & Johnson, 2006). Nagar (2018) also shows, light-skinned people are better off financially and often live in better neighborhoods than dark-skinned people. Consequently, today, after the era of colonialism, there is an increased understanding, acknowledgment, and alas, acceptance of Western standards of beauty in African cultures and other societies around the world (Hunter, 2011; Peltzer, Pengpid, & James, 2016). It is no wonder whiteness is now a leading international capitalist beauty ideal, selling more products than any other, and I doubt that the end of this is anywhere near if skin color remains to be a major criterion when individuals are evaluated in various aspects of society, including choosing a marital partner (Haq, 2013).

Africans Revolutionizing African-ness

Even though skin color and other aspects of what it means to be African have negatively affected many Africans and other people of color around the world, I wish to indulge you on a few who have revolutionized the black identity, although, I must add, it was not easy and didn't happen overnight. I present the former president of the United States of America, Barack Hussein Obama, the late Dr. Maya Angelou, the late Nelson Mandela, and the late Dr. John Pombe Magufuli. These four transcended the negative African story that often showers social media and research studies around the world. I chose Barack Obama because of his African descent. Specifically, his father was Barack Obama Sr. of Kenya, and Ann Dunham of Wichita, Kansas, who met while they were students at the University of Hawaii. Dr, Maya Angelou, on the other hand, offers a complicated astounding story of a strong African woman overcoming obstacles as an African American, while Nelson Mandela and Dr. John Pombe Magufuli shed light on how an African can revolutionize the African mindset by action and by doing so, overcoming local and global limitations to make positive changes in Africa.

Barack Hussein Obama

Barack Hussein Obama II is the first African American president of the United States of America; he served as the forty-fourth president from 2009 to 2017. He is a retired attorney, an American politician, and an author. From 1997 to 2004, he served as a U.S. senator from Illinois and from 2005 to 2008 as an Illinois state senator. Mr. Obama has published three bestselling books, namely, *Dreams from My Father* (1995), *The Audacity of Hope* (2006) and *A Promised Land* (2020). I draw from Obama's book, *Dreams from My Father*, whereby Mr. Obama himself recounts his life experience from a young age to his professional life. His mother and father divorced when he was very young, and he had to go stay with his grandmother in Hawaii because better education opportunities were there. Mr. Obama essentially grew up without his Kenyan father. After his parents divorced in 1963, he saw his father once more in 1971. He learned much about his father from stories told by his mother and grandmother.

He attended Punahou School, a private college-preparatory school where he was one of six black students, and continued studies there until graduation in 1979. It is during his years at Punahou he met Ray (Keith Kakugawa), a multiracial friend who introduced him to the African American community.

Obama recounts a time in his life when he was trying to reconcile the terms of his birth, which divided heritage with realities of race and tribal identity that existed not only in America but also in other parts of the world. At one of his public readings at the Cambridge Public library titled, *Dreams from My Father: A Story of Race and Inheritance,* Obama recited a portion of his book where he remembers times during his adolescent years in Hawaii when issues of race tensions were very high. He shows his struggle in trying to understand his identity, particularly what it really means to be a black man in America. In those years, white friends would often invite one or two black friends to their parties. So, one day he invited a few of his white friends to attend a party with black friends. To his surprise, after just a few minutes, they felt very uncomfortable. After talking to Ray about what happened, Obama reflects on the reality of race and power. He notes,

> "I had begun to see a new map of the world, one that was
> frightening in its simplicity, suffocating in its implications.
> We were always playing on the white man's court, Ray
> had told me, by the white man's rules. If the principal, or
> the coach, or a teacher, or Kurt, wanted to spit in your
> face, he could, because he had power and you didn't. If he
> decided not to, if he treated you like a man or came to your
> defense, it was because he knew that the words you spoke,
> the clothes you wore, the books you read, your ambitions
> and desires, were already his. Whatever he decided to do,
> it was his decision to make, not yours, and because of that

fundamental power he held over you, because it preceded and would outlast his individual motives and inclinations, any distinction between good and bad whites held negligible meaning" (Obama, 1995, p. 85).

Additionally, Obama illustrates how his family, particularly his grandmother and grandfather, exhibited a sense of varied understanding and even comfortability being around black people. For example, his grandmother spoke of how she was frightened one time because a black man asked her for money when she was waiting for a bus. After talking to his grandfather, Obama learned that his grandmother was asked for money by strange men before, but this time she seemed frightened because it was a black man. Obama's grandfather was not happy that his wife was afraid of black people. You can imagine how troubling it must have been for Obama. On the one hand, he is a black African; on the other hand, he is white, raised by two white middle Americans. If even a family with a black grandchild struggled to accept those who looked like their own grandchild, how more complicated is it for other people to deal with issues of race.

Fast forward, years later, Obama completes his education, becomes a prominent politician in America, runs for president and wins. His victory transformed how people in America and around the world see and think about Africans and African Americans in particular. Obama won the American presidency mainly because the American people focused on traits that went beyond race. For example, Debbie White (2020) notes Obama won based on the following factors: empathy and genuine help for Middle-Class Americans, steady leadership, calm temperament as the Los Angeles Times noted: "We need a leader who demonstrates thoughtful calm and grace under pressure, one not prone to volatile gesture or capricious pronouncement . . . as the presidential race draws to its conclusion, it is Obama's character and temperament that come to the fore. It is his steadiness. His maturity." Additionally, he gained the presidency because of his plan to improve healthcare, withdrawal of combat troops from Iraq, and choosing Joe Biden as running mate. Such character traits and choices were critical to him transcending his African-ness. Obama demonstrated the possibilities that go beyond being an African. He underscored qualities that people look for and admire, and in the right moment and at the right time, an African can be what anybody could dream of being. Obama reminds us that we are human first before we are African.

Dr. Maya Angelou

Dr. Maya Angelou was a famous African American woman with many astounding accomplishments, including two NAACP outstanding literary work (nonfiction) image awards given in 2005 and 2009. She wrote thirty-six books and some cookbooks. Angelou was born in St. Louis, Missouri in 1928. Her original name was Marguerite Annie Johnson.

She had a very challenging upbringing. After her parents divorced when she was two, she and her older brother Bailey had to go live with their father's mother in Arkansas. While living in Arkansas, she experienced a lot of prejudice and discrimination as an African American. In addition, at age seven, she was raped by her mother's boyfriend while visiting her mother; because of this traumatic experience, she stopped talking. Despite her difficult childhood, she excelled in so many ways, overcoming every obstacle that came her way. In her early years of adulthood, she became the first black female streetcar conductor in California. In 1952, Maya Angelou married a Greek sailor named Anastasios Angelopoulos, and changed her original name to this professional name, for which she became known. In the 1960s, Angelou lived in Egypt and later in Ghana as a writer, instructor at the University of Ghana, and became part of the pan Africanism movement, which led her to join other black nationalist leaders such as Malcolm X in 1964 upon her return to the United States of America. In the era of World War II, Angelou moved to California after receiving a scholarship to study dance and acting. From that training, her career took off and she was nominated for a Tony award in the play *Look Away* (1973) and another award for her role in the miniseries *Roots* (1977), to name but a few.

I wish to turn our attention to her books, specifically, *I Know Why the Caged Bird Sings* (1969). She penned it under great advice from her fellow writer, James Baldwin, who encouraged her to share her life experiences with the world. Thus, the book is somewhat a memoir detailing her childhood and young adult years where she recounts how she felt from the inside out. The book was such a phenomenal nonfiction best seller ever written by an African American woman. Consequently, Angelou became an international star, and the book is still among the most popular autobiographical works. The audacity to share the most difficult experiences of her life in ways that brings critical aspects of humanity to the forefront made it possible for the book to transcend her race. The memoir welcomed everyone to see sorrow, defeat, helplessness, anguish, despair, and disappointment as a pathway to freedom. Readers of all races— black and white, rich and poor, young and old—only saw ways in which a caged soul can still thrive and touch humanity in a special way. Readers couldn't care about who wrote the book; they only focused on the message in the book. Angelou revolutionized not only how African Americans were perceived, but she also opened a way, a unique way, for the world to understand and learn from those who have suffered but are still willing to find joy and success in life so much that they change the world. In addition to her books, Maya Angelou allowed her strings of struggles and challenges to piece together beads of strength through many poems and essay collections. It is no wonder President Bill Clinton invited her to recite a poem at his 1993 inaugural ceremony, namely, "*On the Pulse of Morning*." Below is a short excerpt.

> A Rock, A River, A Tree, Hosts to species long since departed,
> Marked the mastodon, The dinosaur, who left dried tokens
> Of their sojourn here, On our planet floor,
> Any broad alarm of their hastening doom, Is lost in the gloom
> of dust and ages.
> But today, the Rock cries out to us, clearly, forcefully,
> Come, you may stand upon my, Back and face your distant
> destiny,
> But seek no haven in my shadow, I will give you no hiding
> place down here.
> You, created only a little lower than, The angels, have crouched
> too long in
> The bruising darkness, Have lain too long, Facedown in
> ignorance,
> Your mouths spilling words, Armed for slaughter.
> The Rock cries out to us today, You may stand upon me,
> But do not hide your face. [. . .]

A close examination of this poem shows a call to humanity to be accountable, collaborate, face obstacles, and not to ignore challenges around us. One of my favorite poems by Angelou is "Still I Rise." In this poem, Angelou summons a side of humanity known to every person on the face of the earth. She paints the ugly picture of the human soul that celebrates the defeat and anguish of another soul. Like talking to those who wish her defeat, Angelou sends a message to every person under the sun to anticipate hate, jealousy, and malicious spirit wishing to harm anyone wanting to shine. Angelou calls everyone to believe and know that the negativity around us is not a reason to succumb to defeat. Angelou is speaking to all people; she is talking to humanity to acknowledge an inescapable reality; she is awakening a bold and resilient spirit to everyone and anyone willing to listen. While drawing from the history of oppression and despair, Angelou gives hope a new definition, a new face, and a new destiny. With a poem such as this, she transcended her race. She writes,

"You may write me down in history
With your bitter, twisted lies,
You may trod me in the very dirt
But still, like dust, I'll rise.
　　Does my sassiness upset you?
　　Why are you beset with gloom?
　　'Cause I walk like I've got oil wells
　　Pumping in my living room.
　　Just like moons and like suns,
　　With the certainty of tides,
　　Just like hopes springing high,
　　Still I'll rise.
Did you want to see me broken?
Bowed head and lowered eyes?
Shoulders falling down like teardrops,
Weakened by my soulful cries?
　　Does my haughtiness offend you?
　　Don't you take it awful hard
　　'Cause I laugh like I've got gold mines
　　Diggin' in my own backyard.
You may shoot me with your words,
You may cut me with your eyes,

You may kill me with your hatefulness,
But still, like air, I'll rise.
    Does my sexiness upset you?
    Does it come as a surprise
    That I dance like I've got diamonds
    At the meeting of my thighs?
    Out of the huts of history's shame
    I rise
Up from a past that's rooted in pain
I rise
I'm a black ocean, leaping and wide,
Welling and swelling I bear in the tide.
Leaving behind nights of terror and fear
I rise
Into a daybreak that's wondrously clear
I rise
Bringing the gifts that my ancestors gave,
I am the dream and the hope of the slave.
I rise
I rise
I rise."

Maya Angelou, *"Still I Rise" from "And Still I Rise: A Book of Poems.*
Copyright © 1978 by Maya Angelou.

Dr. John Pombe Magufuli

Both former President Barack Obama and the late Dr. Maya Angelou are African Americans, thus Africans in the diaspora. While their accomplishments are significant, they still don't paint a complete picture, or rather somewhat a balanced portrait of Africans revolutionizing the world's perception of Africans. This distinction is critical because some may argue that the ability to excel in ways illustrated by Africans in the diaspora, such as Obama and Angelou, is only possible when Africans leave their motherland. In other words, it is easy to connect positive aspects of Africans when they are removed from Africa, which in turn could mean, African culture and traditions create an environment and mindset that leads to negative traits that are impossible to overcome until one is removed from it, re-cultured. Therefore, although many Africans have accomplished so much for their countries and the continent at large, first, I briefly underscore specific character traits that allowed the former president of South Africa, the late Nelson Mandela, to change the world by a sheer spirit of courage and unselfishness covered with humility, intelligence, and wisdom.

Mandela was born in 1918, in former British territory South Africa, in a small village known as Transkei. Even though he was one man, through his initiatives, he changed lives, led a nation, and inspired many people around the world. First, because he knew the power of one, he showed that a single person could be a catalyst to bring change. Many times, he was quoted saying, "There's no passion to be found playing small—in settling for a life that is less than the one you are capable of living" (NA, July 2018). Second, Mandela refused to give up on his country and his people. He believed that his freedom could not be separated from that of his fellow countrymen. Even more, he used that struggle to call the world to justice. Third, he was ready to speak up for the sick. Specifically, he fought against the prevalence of HIV/AIDS in South Africa. Fourth, Mandela used his life philosophy and lessons of Ubuntu in ways that allowed the world to partake of them. As Obama put it during his eulogy, "His recognition that we are all bound together in ways that are invisible to the eye; that there is a oneness to humanity; that we achieve ourselves by sharing ourselves with others and caring for those around us . . . He not only embodied Ubuntu, but he also taught millions to find that truth within themselves." Thus, his African-ness was the foundation of what he believed to be right for his own people but also the rights for everyone with blood running in their veins. His character brought a unique perspective to the world that rarely understood what an African is willing to do and can do within the confines of his race while stepping outside of the box to create the freedom that happens only by taking action that reflects positive values of humanity.

Late president of South Africa, Nelson Mandela

I wish to highlight the late Dr. John Pombe Magufuli, the former president of my home country of Tanzania, for two main reasons: one, he is a Sukuma, an ethnic group I presented in chapter 4, but also because he was a current president, thus, demonstrating recent accomplishments of Africans in Africa and beyond. His excellency, the late John Pombe Joseph Magufuli, was a visionary leader for a thriving and progressive Tanzania. I must start by acknowledging that anyone following the politics in Africa and particularly in Tanzania and around the world in general, is fully aware that Magufuli enjoyed both praises and criticism due to his unique, daring, sharp, uncompromising, unapologetic, forceful, and no-nonsense type of attitude throughout his career. That is why he was nicknamed "bulldozer."

As a Sukuma, he displayed the typical hard-working mentality "hapa kazi tu" and a caring spirit typical of many Sukumas. On the other hand, he defies these cultural and traditional norms by being direct, "saying it like it is," and not worrying about the "*mhola*"—peace with those who were responsible and needed to be held accountable in their positions. He didn't waiver. He didn't worry about who to confront, and he didn't mind being criticized or threatened by anyone within the country, continent, and even abroad. I believe history may judge Magufuli more harshly for how he accomplished his goals than for what he accomplished. Whether you agree with his tactics and way of leadership, one thing everybody cannot deny is the fact that he got so much done in such a short period of time.

Magufuli achieved so much partly because he did what most African leaders have been unable to do, namely, identifying problems and addressing them by using a cultural and contextual approach, social-lingual appropriated strategy, and local resources inherently present but were not being used appropriately. Even more, Magufuli was educated in African schools, but he got his further studies abroad. Most Western-educated leaders have used strategies and ideas reflective of what the rest of the world is doing or somewhat Western-approved ideas to combat problems such as poverty. Magufuli didn't just talk about the problems entrenched in his beloved country of Tanzania. He came up with practical strategies to address them. More importantly, I must add, Magufuli paved the way to ask others to contribute positively to the various needs ignored for many years by leading by example.

First, the cultural and contextual approach involved identifying specific problems that could be addressed through proper leadership and speedy solution. For example, he eliminated many ghost workers who continued to eat away money from the government. This approach was contextual because it relied on identifying specific areas, with the help of certain people who held critical positions to address this matter. It was culturally appropriate because he sought counsel and involved others in implementing his strategy. If you may recall, the Sukuma people are very communal. When one person in a village is in need, his family, friends, neighbors, and others come to his or her rescue. Likewise, when Magufuli visited schools, for example, teachers and students told him many problems they faced and needs that had not been met. To address each challenge, he identified who was responsible and examined if the problem would be resolved without any other intervention. In some incidences, he fired government officials instantly. This approach was very popular to many citizens but not for some leaders who feared losing their jobs; some critics felt he was violating human rights and outright embarrassing leaders. If money was needed to build such things as toilets at a specific school, Magufuli held an instant call for others to give toward the cause. He had the audacity to do so because he gave first before asking anybody else to contribute. Even more, he stayed in tune with various aspects of his people to truly understand and address critical needs. For instance, according to the *LifeGate* newspaper post on January 26, 2016, instead of holding big celebrations during the Independence Day (December 9), in the wake of a big cholera outbreak in Dar es salaam, Magufuli encouraged Tanzanians to work together to keep their workplaces, homes, cities, and the country clean, safe, and healthy; he was the first president to go in the streets of Dar es Salaam (Tanzania's capital city) to pick off rubbish. Such action motivated many Tanzanians to do the same.

Second, he used what I call a social-lingual appropriated strategy—meaning he made an effort to connect with his fellow Tanzanians in tangible ways. As such, he came from humble beginnings and made sure to tell his story to connect with many people in poverty. He was a former schoolteacher who later became an industrial chemist and worked as minister of labor. His father was a peasant farmer. He said, "Our home was grass thatched and like many boys, I

Late President of Tanzania, Dr. John Pombe Joseph Magufuli

was assigned to herd cattle, as well as selling milk and fish to support my family" (African heritage, 2021). He was known as a down-to-earth leader who was chosen to serve the people. Considering this background, he didn't mind using the rapid transit bus for transportation. He visited hospitals to examine the quality of health services, danced and sang with artists, listened to many widows in search of justice after losing their husbands, and fought for those in need. He had integrity, which was evident prior to becoming president. He oversaw the program to build good roads in Tanzania. This position gave him access to earn a lot of money if he wanted to, but he didn't. Even more, he fought against corruption and wasteful spending to provide services to those in need. Many critics acknowledge that fighting corruption led him to lose many of his friends. He sacrificed his own money for the good of the country. The emerging market newspaper, Fumbuka Ng'wanakilala (October 4, 2017), notes, "President John Magufuli has revealed he earns a salary of nine million Tanzanian shillings ($4,000) per month, making him one of the lowest-paid African leaders as he pursues a much-criticized policy of deep public spending cuts." People may only appreciate this sacrifice by considering how much African leaders make. Ng'wanakilala (2017) explains,

> By contrast Kenya's president earns a monthly salary of around $14,000. Jacob Zuma of South Africa is paid around $20,000 monthly, following a salary increase by parliament in 2015. Since 2009, Zuma has been embroiled in numerous scandals and allegations of abuse of office, including more than $500,000 of improper state spending on security at his private home. Others with more modest pay include President Muhammadu Buhari of Nigeria, who took a 50 percent pay cut when he took office in May 2015. The annual presidential salary was previously set at 14.1 million naira, which in mid-2015 was the equivalent of $70,000.

Magufuli's commitment to bring accountability and demonstrate mindful spending was well shown when he decided to take a salary cut as mentioned before but was criticized for slashing salaries of state-owned companies' executives to 15 million Tanzanian shillings ($6,700) a month, still more than his own. In the same spirit, he restricted foreign travel accordingly.

Linguistically, Magufuli honored, valued, and elevated African languages. Whenever he traveled around the country, he greeted people using their local languages. He was known to use many languages when he visited big cities known to have people who speak various indigenous African languages. More importantly, he made efforts to bring value and commodify Swahili in a special way. He was proud to be African, he was proud of his culture, he was proud of his language, and he was proud of his identity.

Third, Magufuli channeled Tanzania's local resources to facilitate economic growth. According to Penresa (2019), Magufuli improved the transportation system to facilitate internal and external trade and other commercial activities. Consequently, export and import from neighboring countries increased tremendously. He repaired and renewed the railway system while venturing into building airport terminal three at Julius Nyerere International Airport (JNIA); this project was completed in May 2019, raising the proposed amount to 6.5 million passengers annually, more than twice the current amount. Additionally, through the government's own funds, eight new aircrafts were acquired to revive the airline market in Tanzania. Also, Tanzania no longer imports fossil fuels; rather, it uses its own domestic natural gas reserves, therefore, saving $4 billion between 2015 and 2017, and hence vastly hastening domestic economic output and abilities. The late president also tackled the mining industry. According to *Africa Business Magazine* (August 3rd, 2017),

"Magufuli accused mining companies in the country of not paying their fair share because of favourable contracts. The accusation was, in the minds of many in the East African nation, verified when a committee appointed by the president claimed that Acacia Mining, a subsidiary of Canadian mining company Barrick Gold, had understated its mineral exports over several years by billions of dollars . . . The reforms] are a genuine and legitimate attempt at ensuring that Tanzania gets the best deal from the country's natural resources. Every country in the world wants to maximize the amount they collect through natural resources . . . In Norway, for example, oil contracts are scrutinized by the country's parliament to make sure that they are signing the best deal. I think it's only fair that Tanzania does the same."

Even more, Magufuli invested in human capital, thus making public primary and secondary education free to all children. As a result, in primary schools, students' enrollment increased to 35.2%, while for secondary level, one enrollment increased by 20.1%. I must add, Magufuli was the first president to elect a female vice-president, which in turn, after his death, led to Samia Suluhu Hassan becoming the first woman to become Tanzania's president. Magufuli was more loved by his Tanzanian countrymen and women than those in Western countries; he wanted Africans to be self-reliant and to believe in their ability to prosper independently. His relationship with his fellow Africans and Western economies can be summed up in the following statement: "It is possible to get Africans out of poverty! All that is needed is visionary leaders who love their own . . . who love their fellow humans and not just their pockets! As always, we need to remember not to fall into the trap of democracy [Africans and the Trap of Democracy] laid out by the West, where democracy is a word used by the West against any government which does not abide by their will and does not sell out to them . . ." (African heritage, March 22, 2021).

At the end of his life, Magufuli was criticized for his handling of the coronavirus. He called on Tanzanians to fast and pray, use traditional medicine, and refused to put the country on lockdown. Although data seems to indicate that his approach didn't necessarily cause innumerable deaths compared to neighboring countries such as Kenya, which decided to put its people on lockdown, the international community was not happy about this decision because it was different, unique, daring, and non-conforming. I'm not saying this was right or wrong. All I'm saying is that Magufuli transcended African-ness. He looked from within his country to meet the needs of his people. He awakened Tanzanians to see their value, to see the wealth that God had given them, and to believe that they have the power to bring positive change and lift up their country if they choose to do so. Such audacity is one of a kind, one that history will continue to remember.

Conclusion

In this book, I examined the meaning and various categories of identity. I also presented the definition, levels, and development of culture. Even more, the description and ideology of language were also presented. Such topics laid a foundation to understand ways in which Africans had their own culture and identity prior to foreign contact, while the synthesis of such ideas demonstrated ways in which colonial dominion played a great role in shaping and reshaping African's way of thinking about their own identity. Furthermore, key examples of African culture, such as that of the Sukuma, were presented to not only show aspects of African culture but also give tangible meaning and context on ideas and behaviors rooted in African culture but could be misunderstood and misinterpreted by an outside observer. Social-economic factors such as poverty also play a role in shaping and reshaping a person's identity, as such, circumstances such as the loss of a parent may alter a person's perspective in life, limit their possibilities to excel socially and economically, and in turn may need support to overcome and even transcend their current situation. When that happens, an outside observer with a limited understanding of what's going on may easily judge harshly and negatively those struggling. In fact, the loss of freedom, which is what happened to Africans after colonization, is like losing a father or a parent; it changes, limits, hinders, and distorts various aspects of life. For an outsider, Africans may look like needy children who need assistance, but the reason for their need may be completely misunderstood. Even more, any efforts they make may be completely misjudged if all factors and circumstances surrounding their struggle are not considered. What complicates identity issues for Africans is that others, after such long struggles, see African-ness as synonymous with poverty or shame. They equate their struggles with their identity and, even more, without knowing, they decide to dishonor or even distance themselves from their own identities.

In this book, I have shown you that being an African is being a human. I hope you understand when the world questions critical aspects of identity, when the world ranks various manifestations of what it means to live in the world, the result is people ranking humanity, when we are all human. By examining aspects such as naming and skin color, one sees the universality of what all people have in common. Likewise, the diversity in the context, meaning the insignificance of those aspects differs exponentially. For Africans, identity is never removed from the color of our skin. But the good news is that, even when people from all walks of life acknowledge that we are Africans, one thing cannot be denied, a good person, one with good intentions, one who works hard, one who is selfless, one who is humble, one who is hardworking is valuable to everyone, and for that, even Africans contribute to making the world a better place. Former President Barack Obama, the late Dr. Maya Angelou, the late president of South Africa, Nelson Mandela, and the late former president of Tanzania, Dr. John Pombe Magufuli, have shown that people look for qualities that transcend race and color, and when they do so, even Africans shine and become a role model for others to emulate. This is Africa's identity revolution.

The understanding of our equality as people is key to honoring and valuing our diverse identities. Just because the world questions the value of African indigenous languages in the global market, it doesn't mean the languages cease to have value. Just because the world questions the need to teach indigenous languages and use them in school, it doesn't mean the languages are not needed anymore. In fact, when you are in a village in Ilumba or Ng'wakata wanting to buy a piece of land belonging to a Sukuma farmer, your knowledge of Sukuma language and culture is critical to this transaction; the farmer could care less about your knowledge of English, French, Spanish, or German. At that point, the language you need is Sukuma. Thus, ranking languages using historical, national, and even global economic yardsticks distorts the need and reason for language use. I hope you see how and why many Africans and the world have bought into the mentality and perspective that looks down on Africans. The indigenous African names and naming practices have value; even more, dark skin color is beautiful and is to be cherished rather than despised. Consequently, when I hear someone say Africans are poor and they will never get out of their poverty because they can't think for themselves; they are too corrupt, they are too violent, they're not innovative, they are too dependent on wealthy nations, and they are too lazy, I say look at history, examine politics and the heart of humanity.

To the people in this world, and to my fellow Africans in particular, please hear: a story was told: the donkey told the tiger the grass is blue. The tiger replied, "No, the grass is green." The discussion became heated, and the two decided to submit the issue for arbitration. So, they approached Judge Lion. As they approached the lion on his throne, the donkey started screaming, "Your highness, isn't it true that the grass is blue?" The lion replied, "If you believe the grass is blue, then the grass is blue." The donkey rushed and continued, "The tiger disagrees with me, contradicts me, annoys me, please punish him." The king then declared, "The tiger will be punished, three days of silence," he declared. Well, the donkey jumped and went on his way, content, and repeated, "The grass is blue, the grass is blue." Well, in private the tiger asked the lion, "Your majesty, why have you punished me? After all the grass is green." The lion replied, "You have known and seen, the grass is green." So, the tiger asked, "Why do you punish me?" The lion replied, "That has nothing to do with whether the grass is blue or green. The punishment is because it is degrading, for a brave, intelligent creature like you, to waste time arguing with an ass, and on top of that, you came and bothered me with that question just to validate something you already knew was true. You see, the biggest waste of time is arguing with a fool or fanatic who doesn't care about the truth or reality but only the victory of his or her own beliefs or illusions; never waste time on discussions that make no sense. \Some people, for all the evidence presented to them, do not have the ability to understand nor do they want to understand. They just want to argue. Some are blinded by ego, hatred, and resentment, and they only want to be right—even if they're not. The saying goes, when ignorance screams, intelligence moves on. When Africans move on, our strength shines; this is the African identity revolution. The poem below captures my call for a revolutionized Africa.

Wake up, Africa, the Time Has Come

Africa, you're beautiful beyond measure.

Africans you are worth more than you'll ever know.

The uniqueness of your culture and the beautiful
 names of your children and grandchildren are
 adorable, like a diamond ring.

Since centuries ago, many came from a far searching
 for your riches.

Why'd you look down on yourself.

For decades, kings and queens traveled to fight for you,
 just to get what you have.

You have survived and tamed the furious tragedies that
 came swept your land

you survived and thrived for centuries without aid.

Why don't you believe you're more than what the
 world tells?

Why does everyone sell your properties, your fabrics,
   your food, your minerals and get rich because you
   buy chemicals to be white? Don't you remember
   your strength before slavery? You have shown the
   world the power of an African; you have shown
   humanity you can overcome whatever the world
   brings your way.
Look at your land, look at your people, look at their
   heart, see the joy that African children display even
   when they don't have a single cent in their pocket.
Listen to them emit peace letting them enjoy what the
   world offers.
Look at the African mother surrounded by her sisters
   and aunts to cook for her when her baby is born.
   Look at the ceremony the elders perform to
   welcome the African child who comes to make
   a mark in the world. Do you really think being
   African is not good? Do you really believe their
   lie? Have you really stopped dreaming of a new
   tomorrow?
Wake up Africa,
the grass is still green.
your land has gold
your people have power
Wake up Africa
the world is watching
they are turning around, you're moving forward
why listen to the whispers of doom?
when can you smile at the singing of the birds?
match with a fist of sweet revenge
lift your foot one after the other, stand tall and shout
I am the son of strength

I am the daughter of beauty
My yard drips of diamond
I am alive and awake
Just watch me thrive
Hear my people roar like a lion hunting
Read the pages of history of my wise ruling
Changing my name doesn't erase my being
Though strangled with the darkness of the night
With the dawn of a new day shining like rays from
    above
I am awake
I will walk softly and boldly like an aunt in the
    elephant's trunk
I will bite sharply the deceptions of the world till the
    giant's lies fall
Wake up Africa
I hear your thunder
I hear you now.

Reflections

Sample Letters from Students' Reflections Based on Lessons Learned from Topics Explored

Letter 1: A Letter to My Mother

Dear Mom,

I wish you would be more open to learning about racism. I know you like to think you're not racist, that you "don't see color." But it's so important to see color! Our skin color does define us. If you pretend it doesn't, you won't see the things that need to be changed in our world. You see a black woman with an afro and you tell me she looks unprofessional, but why? You need to think about how we have been led to believe what is natural to [us] should be natural to everyone.

The white way is not the only way. Just because the white methods for everything are newer does not mean modern ways are better or more civilized than traditional methods. When my sisters or I leave our hair curly, you tell us it looks like a mess. But when my hair fell out after spending three years straightening it every day, you didn't like that either! Why did you marry a Jewish man if you didn't love what made him who he is? You see a black man killed after his neck is knelt on for eight straight minutes by a white cop, a man whose sole job is to protect citizens, and you say nothing. You see a cop car set on fire on the news and then you say something! How can you only condemn violence when it comes from the oppressed? You claim you don't see color but clearly, you identify with the cop. Why would you defend them so vehemently if you "don't see color"? This class I have taken has taught me that western values shouldn't be all that matters. Hatred based on skin color is appealing and horrible, but our race does matter. Black people face struggles you and I could never imagine. So do Asian people, and Hispanic people, and every other race and ethnicity there is. As white women, we need to learn about racism so we know how to combat it and correct our own actions. If you claim to not see color, you cannot see the injustices all these groups face. Please, mother, I am begging you to better yourself. I sent you a list of anti-racism resources to educate yourself so you could do better, and instead of thinking about yourself and reflecting on how could you change to help combat racism, you instead screamed at me and called me disrespectful for "calling you a racist," which I never did. If we fail to teach ourselves about issues black people face, and the history of these issues, we will never grow. This bass has taught me the history of apartheid, how westernization has ruined traditional African values, how class, race, and gender issues often go hand in hand. As a woman, can't you sympathize with black women? As a woman from a poor family, why can't you empathize with poor black people? If you are willing to listen, I can show you what I have learned to help you not be complicit in these issues. This course has taught me to identify with people of every background, to wish for their accomplishments and mourn their failures. This class has allowed me to see through the eyes of poor African children, of white parents that hate their black children. I have learned the terrors of segregation and apartheid, and how racism is such a deeply ingrained view in American life and all of western civilization. Even one of our presidents has faced racism in his life. It's a very important issue, and we need to do all we can to learn about it and speak up for silenced voices. Mom, please let me help you so you can help others. It's not an attack on you or your pride to learn what is wrong and what you can do to correct it. I am begging you, please let me teach you. If you continue to choose this willful ignorance, to pretend that race doesn't matter and racism isn't real, you will actively contribute to keeping racism alive. You make fun of your father for being outdated and stubbornly refusing to change his views, yet you are following the same fate. Thank you for raising me to think critically and challenge every idea I encounter. You raised me to stand up for myself and to speak for what is right, so now you have to trust me when I try to help you. You were so proud of me for getting into this school. Please let me share all that I have learned with you.

Letter 2: A Letter to My Roommate

Hey Jane (pseudonym)

I am writing this letter encouraging you to consider joining the class I've told you all about. A lot of our recent conversations were in particular about the need for Americans to be involved and aware of the different cultures and allow ourselves to be immersed. To tell you a little about why I think it is so important to be educated is because of the racial trauma, or trauma itself of experiencing two different cultures, and essentially two different lives, and from it, people experience anger.

People use their emotions to let others know how they would like to express and one way they do this is through anger. Anger itself is nothing new as it is the root of what allows people to speak up and for those who would rather bottle their emotions whereas others will express themselves to allow their surroundings to know what they are feeling. Anger that festers for a while, as was previously stated, is at its root what is shown. It is what is found deeper under that anger that we realize the true nature of this world and how it does not give space for people to process that anger. Anger is only a surface-level emotion because what is deeply rooted in the anger stems from previous pain, frustration, and people's inability to speak up for themselves. While some people think they are to blame for not speaking up about the issues festering in their hearts and mind, people fail to consider that the media and platforms we use to receive news choose to ignore certain issues keep themselves from being backed down by supporters. For those who self-censor their own emotions, this causes them to feel trapped as they are not able to express their feelings. With the start of just one person speaking up, this influences the people around them to do the same in a sort of domino effect. This effect can help people who do not know how to use their own voice know that sharing can start a trend and theme of people sticking up for each other, even in the midst of self-censorship in government form. In a society in which it is free, the people must be able to set their goals and think for themselves. In America, people are at an advantage of speaking up for themselves and expressing their ideas. Even if the topic is unpopular or controversial, they are still able to voice out their opinions and participate in peaceful protest. Because of these benefits, people can discuss and debate rather than being censored and punished. The cause of self-censorship can be so damaging as it can ruin the lives of others and the fear that millennials impact the way they act today. Every social group has its own opinion when it comes to values and beliefs, but those who do not show their views are usually dealing with self-esteem and confidence issues from col-leagues or people they generally like to surround themselves with. Even though Americans are given freedom of speech, people today still self-censor themselves because of the way others will react. It is generally easier to bottle the opinions people have rather than expressing themselves because the outcome of speaking out can go in two different ways. People need to start learning what it is like to stick up for themselves and for others because when they don't, we are not keeping people in power accountable and calling them out on the harm they have done and will continue to do.

As important as it is to recognize our anger and address our problems, it is just as important for us as individuals to be edu-cated enough to speak up on the oppression of the American people. While many claim that "Ignorance is bliss," this phrase does more harm than any good anyone can ever think of. Choosing to stay ignorant to important issues shows the privilege some people have, knowing that the oppression and suppression of people's ideals do not pertain to their personal life. Education is important, and while it is deeply encouraged that all children strive to achieve a degree of some sort in college, there seems to be a lack of understanding of what is needed to be successful in the United States. While the school system does a great job in teaching their students that work-ing hard is worthwhile and teaches them good prioritization skills, what they fail to teach is that striving to achieve a 9-5 job plays into the idea that having that is what every American wish to achieve. Students are taught about history in the eyes of America and lack the opportunity to see what harm America has done to neighboring countries for their personal gain. This self-censorship ultimately does not allow Americans the freedom to think for themselves but rather think for America as a whole. Individualism is heavily preached and is a proud freedom that Americans hold dear, but our individualism harms different communities and does not teach people living in

America about how important it is to love others who are different. So, when we say "Ignorance is bliss," we are choosing to ignore the pain of other groups, ignore our loved ones when they are hurting, and bring comfort to our own selves.

The reason I speak on the topics of anger and ignorance is because of what I learned in my SWAHILI class. I realize how important it is to be educated about different cultures, the problems arising in them, and how we as a diverse nation can benefit from hearing others' stories. I know you, and I have talked a lot about the injustices of the world but having an actual class with many students and our different cultures allows me to understand the actual need for healing and education. I hope you'll consider taking this class your last year at UGA, and if you can't, I would love it if you could send this to your friend.

Best,

Chikenda

Letter 3: A Letter to My Grandmother

Dear Nani,

Identity is a set of qualities or characteristics that make a person who they are. When I asked you about yours, you could only respond with the identities that other people gave you. At first, I was very frustrated. At first, I wondered how a person could not understand the concept of identity. However, I remembered that you were never given that chance. All your life, you were forced into situations that gave you your identity. You were forced to become a bride and then a mother. You were never allowed to work and build connections with people. All your life, you went along pleasing other people and going with their own flow. As I was growing up, you taught me to do the same. In our culture, women are expected to stay quiet and follow the man's orders. Women were never given a chance in our culture. As much as I love and appreciate our culture, there are some things that I wish we would change. You could even call these cultural social norms. Firstly, I want to touch on the topic of marriage. In our culture, once a girl has reached the age of 18, you begin to look for a husband for her. One of the reasons why many women in our culture understand the concept of self-identity is because they are rushed into marriage. Before they can understand who they are and what they are capable of, they are forced to understand others? Once married, you are no longer a part of your family. In fact, we commonly use the phrase "Giving her away" to describe a young girl's marriage. They are expected to sacrifice everything for their husband and his family. I wish that we could erase this concept. Why should a girl get married before she gets the chance to know herself? It's important to allow a person to explore their abilities. Instead, our culture ties the success of a woman to marriage. A woman is successful if her husband is happy. This is the example you set up for my mother. When we conform to a social norm, it is an example to our children of how normal this norm is. In psychology, one of the reasons why many people do not speak up or fight for change is because they are so used to seeing life one way, they are afraid of what is outside that life. I wish you could understand the importance of establishing an identity, yourself and not allowing others to rule over you. When you mentioned that being a grandmother of four girls was your favorite identity, it finally made me realize that you do have an idea of what identity may be. Since you never were given the chance, you think identity is limited to your male family members. Identity is not limited to being someones' wife or daughter. It is beyond that. The first way you can build your self-identity is by reflecting on yourself. Acknowledge your strengths and weaknesses. You have so many things you can be proud of. Although there is nothing wrong with being a housewife, there is a difference between those who choose it and those who it is forced upon. Your feelings, among many other bangladeshi women's feelings were never acknowledged. No one ever asked what you wanted. It was easy to get you married as if you were a burden. It's time we change that. Stop relying on a man to tell you what you are worth. Build your own identity and own it. Find something that you feel strong about and make it your identity. It's never too late to appreciate yourself for who you are. I want to end by thanking you. Through your life experiences, my sisters and I were able to understand the importance of living to please ourselves. We were able to break out of that shell and live to our own expectations. Thank you for teaching us how to love ourselves and to be proud of our accomplishments. I wish you were able to do the same in your life.

Sincerely,
Your loving granddaughter Zubeida (pseudonym)

SUPPLEMENTAL RESOURCES

- Dreams from My Father – a short presentation of the book: https://www.youtube.com/watch?v=F5k60W6pwv8
- Maya Angelou-Mini biography: https://www.youtube.com/watch?v=LyHqafC740Q
- Skin—film released in 2008, based on the book *When She Was White: The True Story of a Family Divided by Race* by Judith Stone: https://vimeo.com/166163687
- Can you change your race? The Maury show: https://www.youtube.com/watch?v=L1yWH6QSP4k

DISCUSSION QUESTIONS

Watch the following video clip:
https://www.youtube.com/watch?v=F5k60W6pwv8

Answer the following questions and discuss accordingly.

1. Who is this video clip about—name the person?

   _____

   _____

2. How is Obama connected to African ancestry?

   _____

   _____

3. Highlight some of the issues he discusses in this video clip—especially those that deal with identity. Please jot down as many issues as you can.

   _____

   _____

   _____

   _____

   _____

   _____

4. What is the take-away for you from this video clip?

_____

_____

5. Comment on any aspect of this video clip—connections/
   questions/input

_____

_____

Maya Angelou
Watch the following video clip:
https://www.youtube.com/watch?v=LyHqafC740Q

Answer the following questions and discuss accordingly.

1. Did you know Dr. Angelou before watching this clip?
   If so, how?

_____

_____

2. What types of identity did Dr. Angelou experience
   throughout her life?

_____

_____

3. What aspects of her identity surprised you and why?

_____

_____

4. How would you describe Dr. Angelou based on the information you learned?

   _____

   _____

5. Discuss what this video clip made you think about—any aspect you would like?

   _____

   _____

6. Do you know other African American women or other people with many identities throughout their lives? What does this mean to you?

   _____

   _____

7. Comment on anything you would like.

   _____

   _____

INTERVIEW ACTIVITY

Identity-interview guidelines

Take a few minutes to talk to somebody about the following questions and record their answers. After the interview, please write a report on your findings.

Name of interviewer: _____

Name of interviewee: _____

Age: (optional) _____

Gender: _____

Race: _____

Instructions

Introduce yourself and state the purpose of this interview—to learn about people's perceptions or understanding about identity and ways in which their sense of identity has an impact on any aspect of their lives.

Questions to guide your conversation

1. How do you define identity? What is identity?
2. How do you identify yourself?
3. How do others identify you?

4. Do you have more than one identity? If so, which identity matters the most and why, says who? If you only have one, what is it and does it matter to you?
5. How do you feel about who you are?
6. What is the one thing you wish people knew about you? And why?
7. What do you like the most about yourself?
8. Do you have any question(s) to ask me?

Project – Helpful Ideas to Implement Topics and Issues Discussed in This Book
Projects for Small Groups

OPTION 1

In groups of three to six, collaboratively design a critical analysis of the movie *Black Panther* and your views on how this movie addresses issues of identity not only for Africans, African Americans, and other people in general. Be sure to address ideas expressed through the lens of Traditional vs. Modernity. The analysis needs to address issues of identity explored in this course. Conclude your analysis with your opinion on whether this film did a good job or a bad job in its depiction of Africa and its culture(s) and explain why. (Each group member can focus on one of the following: 1). How does the movie address issues of identity for Africans 2)? How does the movie address issue of identity for African Americans 3)? What issues does the movie bring through the lens of modern vs. traditional, for example, clothing, etc. 4). Does this movie do a good job or bad in their depiction of African culture? Think of the tribes the movie presents, such as the type of clothes they wore, or language used, etc. 5). Would you recommend this movie to someone else? If yes, why, and if not, why?

OPTION 2

In groups of three to six, design a survey of not less than five questions soliciting people's input on their perceptions about the films *Black Panther, Coming to America,* or *Skin*. Conduct the survey and record responses from your participants. Discuss your findings considering identity issues explored in the course. Drawing from your findings, do you agree with perceptions expressed by the majority, and if so, why, or why not. And, based on this experience, what questions do you wish you would have asked but didn't and why? As a group, what did you learn from this assignment? Make sure your participants are diverse, i.e., male and female, young and old, various races (if possible) etc. Be sure to decide which role each of you will play in completing the project. For example, each member can contribute one or two survey questions; once you receive the responses, all of you discuss the findings. After this, each member may focus on addressing the guiding questions provided. In the end, your project should have the following: (A). The survey questions you created (B). Write a summary of the responses to the survey questions and whether you (personally or as a group) agree with the responses of most of the people you interviewed (C). Questions you wish to have asked (D). What did you learn from this assignment?

OPTION 3

You may design a five-minute video clip, a PowerPoint with audio input, or a cartoon clip with clear topics/themes addressing a specific issue on identity. You may each design a slide or two and contribute to the entire project, or you may choose to do otherwise but be sure that everyone does their part.

Projects to Be Completed Individually

1. Critique any of the movies/films/video clips discussed in this book, such as *Queen of Katwe, Skin*, and more, do so

from various ideas or concepts of identity—gender, race, social status, skin, hair, education etc. In your critique, be sure to comment on whether you would recommend this movie and why. As you answer that question, give a simple but meaningful analysis of the movie and how it was helpful or not helpful in helping you learn or examine a specific issue or multiple issues of identity.

2. Research more about characters or things explored in a movie. For example, you could research chess clubs in Uganda, the status of Phiona Mutesi, or where the country is right now on issues of gender equality etc.

3. Suggest/recommend at least seven movies you believe each would be useful or helpful in exploring issues we covered in class. Be sure to explain why you feel it would be useful by connecting it to ideas or issues investigated in this book.

4. Write a letter to someone you wish to express any aspect of the issues presented. You could write an apology letter to people you have never spoken to due to specific issues of identity. You could write your parents or grandparents a letter of gratitude, expressing thankfulness for raising you to accept yourself and others. You could write a letter to students to invite them to take a class that delves into a culture different from their own, one that will encourage them to think deeply about their own sense of identity.

5. If gifted with a great voice, you may compose and record a song, a poem, a rap, or a spoken word. You will need to give your composition a clear title. You need an explanation of why you chose to write/compose and what audience you wish to reach. Explain how your song ties to topics or ideas explored in class, especially the issue of identity.

6. Write a reflection paper of your learning by focusing on areas that stood out to you or meant the most. Start with at

least three, but five areas would be a great start. You could identify at least one idea per chapter.

7. Create a cartoon on any topic you would like based on what we explored in this class

8. Write a grant proposal to start a non-profit organization you feel will make a difference in places like Katwe, Uganda. Your proposal needs a title and an introduction of who you wish to write the grant for. You will need to explain the significance or purpose of the grant and the estimated amount requested with a clear explanation of each expense. Lastly, explain how this grant will help your recipients to still value who they are despite their economic or other struggles.

9. Write the author of Song of Lawino & Song of Ocol commenting on any aspect of the book. Write the author of this book, ask questions you wish were addressed or share ideas to add to what was discussed.

10. Create Jeopardy or any game to educate someone about things you learned from this book.

11. If you are a photography major, tap into the aspect of imagery in expressing identity. Please give a brief overview of your art (what is it) and the message intended to be conveyed. Also, identity the issue/topic it is addressing and why you chose to address that issue.

12. Create a simple ABC book with information learned so you may share it with your child, niece/nephew/grandchild, or a friend.

13. Write an article or newspaper article based on any aspect explored in class. Be sure to have a newspaper in mind (to determine the length and style) and to identify the audience you are trying to reach.

14. Come up with your own idea.

REFERENCES

Abrahams, R.G. (1967). The Peoples of Greater Unvamwezi. London: International African Institute.

Abrahams, R. E. (1998). Vigilant Citizens, London: Polity.

Abrams, D. (1999). Social identity and social cognition. In D. Abrams & M. A. Hogg (Eds.), Social identity and social cognition (pp. 197-229). Malden, MA: Blackwell.

Abdelal. R., Herrera. Y.M., Johnston, A. I., & McDermot. R. (2006). Identity as a variable. *Article*, 4 (4), 695-711.

Ade Ajayi, J. F. (1992). Presidential Address in A. Irele (ed.), *African Education and Identity.* Proceedings of the 5th Session of the International Congress of African Studies, Ibadan, December. London & New York: H. Zell Spectrum Books, 21–26.

African heritage. (March 22, 2021). President John Magufuli in His Own Words. Accessed from: https://afrolegends.com/2021/03/22/president-john-magufuli-in-his-own-words/

Allen, B. J. (2011). Difference Matters: Communicating Social Identity, 2nd ed. Long Grove, IL: Waveland.

Al-Sharif, W. (2010). Okot p'Bitek," in Men and Ideas, Jerusalem Academic Publications.

Armingeon, K. (2016). "Political Institutions." In Handbook of Research Methods and Applications in Political Science. (Eds). Keman, H. and Jaap J. W. Cheltenham, UK: Edward Elgar Publishing, 234–47.

Atkinson DR, Brown MT, Parham AT, Matthews LG, Landrum-Brown J, Kim AU. African American client skin tone and clinical judgments of African American and European American psychologists. Professional Psychology. 1996; 27:500–505.

Andreatta, S., & Ferraro, G. (2012). Elements of culture: An applied perspective. Nelson Education.

Angelou, M. (1978). "Still I Rise" from "And Still I Rise: A Book of Poems. Random House

Angelou, M. (1994). "On the Pulse of Morning" (excerpt) from *On the Pulse of Morning*. Collected Poems of Maya Angelou, Random House Inc.

Assié-Lumumba, N.T. (2016). The making of culture and definition of cultural spheres and boundaries in post-colonial Africa: The role of education in acquiring and exercising agency; 4(4), p.18-32.

Baldwin, J.R., Faulkner, S.L., Hecht, M.L., Lindsley, S.L., (2006). Redefining culture: Perspectives across the disciplines. Routledge.

Bekerie, A. (1997). Ethiopic, an African Writing System: Its History and Principles. Lawrenceville, NJ: Red Sea Press.

Berwick, R. C., Friederici, A. D., Chomsky, N., & Bolhuis, J. J. (2013). Evolution, brain, and the nature of language. Trends in Cognitive Sciences, 17(2), 98. http://doi.org/10.1016/j.tics.2012.12.002.

Bessire. M. H.C. (N.D). Sukuma Chiefs and Royal History. Sukuma Museum. Bujora Cultural Centre – Kisesa, Mwanza, Tanzania. Accessed from: http://sukumamuseum.org/sukumachiefs-and-royal-history/

Bernhardt (Samaki), S. (2001). African Names – Reclaim Your Heritage, South Africa: Struik Publisher, 7.

Bickerton, D. (2009). Adam's Tongue. How Humans Made Language, How Language Made Humans. New York: Hill and Wang.

Birley, H. M. (1982). "Resource Management in Sukumaland, Tanzania," Africa: *Journal of the International African Institute*, 52 (2), p. 1-30.

Bierstedt, R. (1970). The Social Order. 3rd edition. McGraw-Hill Book Company.

Bishop, R. S. (2003), "Reframing the Debate about Cultural Authenticity" in D. L. Fox and K. G. Short (eds.), Stories Matter: The Complexity of Cultural Authenticity in Children's Literature. Urbana, IL: *National Council of Teachers of English*, 25–37.

Blohm, W. (1931). The Land of Nyamwezi and Witchcraft, Humburg.

Brock-Utne, B. (2007). Language of instruction and student performance: New insights from research in Tanzania and South Africa. *International Review of Education*, 53, 5/6, 509-530.

Bonder, B.R., Martin, L., Miracle, A.W. (2004). Culture emergent in occupation. *American Journal of Occupational Therapy*, 58(2), p. 159-168.

Botha, R. (2000). Discussing the evolution of the assorted beasts called language. *Language & Communication*, 20, 149–160.

Botha, R. (2003). *Unravelling the Evolution of Language*. Amsterdam: Emerald Group Publishing Limited.

Botha, R. (2006a). On the windows approach to language evolution. *Language & Communication*, 26, 129–43.

Berwick, F., Chomsky, N., & Bolhuis, (2013). Evolution, brain, and the nature of language.

Boyd, R., & Richerson. P. J. (1985). Culture and the Evolutionary Process. Chicago: Chicago University Press.

Bond S, Cash TF. (1992). Black beauty: Skin color and body images among African-American college women. *Journal of Applied Social Psychology.* 22, 874–888.

Bukurura, S. (1994). 'Sungusungu and the banishment of suspected witches in Kahama, Tanzania,' in R.G. Abrahams (ed.), Witchcraft in Contemporary Tanzania, Cambridge: African Studies Centre.

Cann, R. L., Mark S., & Wilson, A. C. (1987). Mitochondrial DNA and Human Evolution, *Nature*, 325, 31–36.

Carmichael S. (2003). Ready For Revolution. New York, NY: Scribner.

Cavanaugh, J.R. (2020). Language ideology revisited. De Gruyter ǀ Published online: April 30, 2020. https://doi.org/10.1515/ijsl-2020-2082

Cavalli-Sforza, L. L., & Feldaman. M. (1981). Cultural Transmission and Evolution: a Quantitative Approach, Princeton: Princeton University Press.

Cavalli-Sforza, L.L., Piazza, A., Menozzi, P., & Mountain, J. (1988). Reconstruction of Human Evolution: Bringing Together Genetic, Archaeological, and Linguistic Data. Proceedings of the National Academy of Sciences, 85(16), 6002-6 DOI:10.1073/pnas.85.16.6002.

Celious A., & Oyserman, D. (2001). Race from the inside: an emerging heterogeneous race Journal of Applied Social Psychology model. *Journal of Social Issues Special Issue: Stigma: An insider's perspective*, 57:149–165.

Charnley, S. (1997). Environmentally-Displace People and the Cascade Effect: Lessons from Tanzania. *Human Ecology*, 25(4), 593-614.

Chebet-Choge, S. (2012). "Fifty Years of Kiswahili in Regional and International Development." *Journal of Pan-African Studies*, 4(10), 172–203.

Chomsky, N. (1972). *Language and mind*. New York: Harcourt Brace Jovanovitch.

Colbert, J.P. (2010). Developing a culturally responsive classroom collaborative of faculty, students, and institution. *Contemporary Issues in Education Research*, 3 (9), 17-29.

Collier, M. J. (1996). Communication Competence Problematics in Ethnic Friendships, *Communication Monographs*, 63 (4), 318.

Dan, M. (2020). Culture as a Multi-Level and Multi-Layer Construct. *Review of International Comparative Management*, 21(2), 226-240.

Eberhardt, J. L., Davies, P. G., Purdie-Vaughns, V. J., & Johnson, S. L. (2006). Looking death worthy: Perceived stereo typicality of black defendants predicts capital sentencing outcomes. Psychological Science, 17, 383-386

Erikson, E. H. (1951). Childhood and society. New York: Norton.

Erikson, E. H. (1968). Identity: Youth and crisis. New York: Norton.

Erez, M., Gati, E. (2004). A dynamic, multi-level model of culture: from the micro level of the individual to the macro level of a global culture. *Applied Psychology*, 53(4), p. 583-598.

Evans, H. E. (1991). Rural-Urban Relations, Household Income Diversification and Agricultural Productivity. *Development and Change.* 22(3), 519-545.

Favareau, D. (2008). The Biosemiotic Turn. *Biosemiotics*, 1(1), 5–23.

Fuggles-Couchman, N. R. (1964). Agricultural Change in Tanganyika: 1945-1960. Stanford California: Stanford University, Food Research Institute.

Fernández, R. (2008). Culture and Economics, in New Palgrave Dictionary of Economics, ed. By S. Durlauf, and L. Blume. Palgrave Macmillan, Basingstoke and New York, 2nd ed.

Fernández, Raquel (2010). Does Culture Matter? IZA Discussion Papers, No. 5122, Institute for the Study of Labor (IZA), Bonn, http://nbn-resolving.de/urn:nbn:de:101:1-201010132778

Fitch, W.T. (2017). Empirical approaches to the study of language evolution. *Psychonomic Bulletin Review*, 24, 3–33.

Fitch, W. T., Huber, L., & Bugnyar, T. (2010). Social Cognition and the Evolution of Language: Constructing Cognitive Phylogenies. *Neuron*, 65(6), 795–814.

Fitzpatrick, L. A. (2012), African Names and Naming Practices: The Impact Slavery and European Domination had on the African Psyche, Identity and Protest. Accessed from African psyche, naming.pdf

Gal, S. (2006). "Contradictions of Standard Language in Europe: Implications for the Study of Practices and Publics." *Social Anthropology*, 14 (2):163–181. https://doi.org/10.1111/j.1469-8676.2006.tb00032.x.

Galaty, J. G. (1988). Pastoral and Agro-pastoral Migration in Tanzania: Factors of Economy, Ecology and Demography in Cultural Perspective.

In Bennett,]. W. &J. R. Bowen (eds.), Production and Autonomy: Anthropological Studies and Critiques of Development. New York: University Press of America, pp. 163-183.

Gates, H. L. (1999). Wonders of the African World. Knopf Doubleday Publishing Group.

Gauvin, L. R. (2013). "In and Out of Culture: Okot p'Bitek's Work and Social Repair in Post Conflict Acoliland," *Oral Tradition*, 28 (1), 35-54)

Gores, V., & Kapinga, O. (2020). The Influence of Roman Catholic Church on the Sukuma Traditional Marriages in Magu District, Tanzania, *Journal of Arts and Humanities*, 9 (3).

Gondo, K. (2010). Language, culture Key Pillars of Development. Herald, February 2010.

Grambs, J. D. (1965). The self-concept: Basis for reeducation of Negro youth. In W. C. Kvaraceus, J. S. Gibson, F. K. Patterson, B. Seasholes, & J. D. Brambs (Eds.), Negro self-concept: Implications for school and citizenship (pp. 11-51). New York, NY: McGraw-Hill.

Gullickson, A. (2005). The significance of color declines: A re-analysis of skin tone differentials in post-Civil Rights America. Social Forces, 84, 157-180.

Hall, E.T., 1989. Beyond culture. Anchor.

Hall, R. (2005). From the Psychology of Race to the Issue of Skin Color for People of African Descent. Journal of Applied Social Psychology. 35, 1958–1967.

Hauser, M., Chomsky, N., & Fitch, W.T. (2002). The faculty of language: what is it, who has it, and how did it evolve? *Science,* 298, 1569–79.

Hankins, T. D. (1974). Response to Drought in Sukumaland, Tanzania. In White, G. F. (ed.), Natural Hazards: Local, National, Global. London: Oxford University Press, pp. 98-104.

Haq, R. (2013). Intersectionality of gender and other forms of identity: Dilemmas and challenges facing women in India. Gender in Management: An International Journal, 28, 171-184.

Heald. S. (2002). Domesticating Leviathan: sungusungu groups in Tanzania. Crisis states programme. Development research center. Working paper no.16.

Helmke, G., & Levitsky, S. (eds.) (2006) Informal Institutions and Democracy. Lessons from Latin America (Baltimore, Johns Hopkins).

Heckler, M., & Birch, C. (1997). Building bridges with stories. In D. A. Leening (ed.), Storytelling Encyclopedia: Historical, cultural, and multiethnic approaches to oral traditions around the world (pp. 8–15). The Oryx Press.

Heron, G. (1976). The Poetry of Okot P'Bitek. Africana Publishing Company.

Hurford, J. R. (2014). *Origins of Language: A Slim Guide.* Oxford: Oxford University Press.

Hungwe, M. J. (2012). "Healing Environmental Harms: Social Change and Sukuma Traditional Medicine on Tanzania's Extractive Frontier." (Natural Resources and Environment) in the University of Michigan: 65–67.

Hill M. (2002a). Skin color and the perception of attractiveness among African Americans: Does gender make a different? Social Psychology Quarterly, 65:75–91.

Hill, J. H. (2009). The Everyday Language of White Racism. Malden, MA: Wiley Blackwell.

Hinkkanen, R. (2009). Someone to welcome you home: Infertility, medicines, and the Sukuma Nyamwezi. Research Series in Anthropology, University of Helsinki.

Hodgson, G. M. (2016). What are institutions? *Journal of Economic Issues*, p. 1-25.

Hofstede, G. (1980), Culture's Consequences: International Differences in Work-Related Values. Newbury Park, CA: Sage.

Hofstede, G., (2001). Culture's consequences: Comparing values, behaviors, institutions, and organizations across nations. Sage publications.

Hofstede, G., Hofstede, G.J., Minkov, M. (2010). *Cultures and Organizations: Software of the Mind*. Revised and expanded 3rd Edition. N.Y: McGraw-Hill.

Hogg, M. A. (2003). Social identity. In M. R. Leary & P. Tangney (Eds.), Handbook of self and identity (pp. 462-479). New York: Guilford Press.

Hosea, J. (2018). Mwanza Town as the Communication Hub of the Lake Zone, 1900-1980, UDSM.

Hunter, M. L. (2005). Race, gender, and the politics of skin tone. New York, NY: Routledge.

IFAD. (2008). Tassa and Soil Fertility in Niger. Rome: IFAD.

Irvine, J. T., & Gal, S. (2000). "Language Ideology and Linguistic Differentiation." In Regimes of Language, edited by P. Kroskrity, 35–84. Santa Fe: School for American Research.

Insaidoo, K.A. (2011). Moral Lesson in African Folktales Authorhouse USA.

Izumi, N. (2017). Agro-Pastoral Large-Scale Farmers in East Africa: A Case Study of Migration and Economic Changes of the Sukuma in Tanzania. *Nilo-Ethiopian Studies*, 22, p. 55-66.

James, W. (1892). Psychology: Briefer course. London, England: Macmillan & Co.

Jütting, J., Drechsler D., Bartsch, S. & de Soysa, I. (eds.) (2007). Informal institutions: How social norms help or hinder development. Paris: OECD.

Kahura, D. (2020). Magufuli's Legacy: The Good, the Bad and the Ugly. The Elephant—Speaking truth to power. Accessed from: https://www .theelephant.info/features/2020/07/25/magufulis-legacy-the-good-the-bad and-the-ugly/

Kapinga, M.O. (2020). Society and its Reproduction: The Case of Wasukuma of Tanzania. The Cradle of Knowledge: *African Journal of Educational and Social Science Research*, 8(1), 35-46.

Kakeya, K. & Sugiyama, Y. (1985). Citemene, Finger Millet and Bemba Culture: A Socio ecological Study of Slash-and-burn Cultivation in

North-eastern Zambia. African Study Monographs, Supplementary Issue, 4, 1-24.

Kaufman, E. A., & Wiese, D. L. (2012). Skin-tone preferences and self-representation in Hispanic children. Early Child Development and Care, 182 (2), 277-290

Kimambo, I., Nyanto, S., & Maddox, G. (2017). A New History of Tanzania, Mkuki na Nyota, Dar es Salaam.

Kimuyu, H. (2016). US Navy band performs 'Baba Yetu' in Swahili and it's astonishing. Nairobi News. Accessed from https://nairobinews.nation.co.ke/chillax/us-navy-band-performs baba-yetu-in-kiswahili-and-its-astonishing.

Kjekshus, H. (1996), Ecology Control and Economic Development in East African History: The Case of Tanganyika1850, Mkuki and Nyota.

Klonoff, E. A., & Landrine, H. (2000). Is skin color a marker for racial discrimination? Explaining the skin color-hypertension relationship. Journal of Behavioral Medicine, 23(4) 329-338.

Koponen, J. (1988). People and Production to the Late19th Century in Tanzania, Finish Historical Society, Helsinki.

Kroeber, A., & C. Kluckhohn. (1952): Culture. Meridian Books, New York.

Kroskrity, P.V. (2000). Regimes of language: Ideologies, polities, and identities. James Currey Publishers. p. 35-83.

Kroskrity, P.V. (2004). Language ideologies. A companion to linguistic anthropology. Volume 496.

Kroskrity, P.V. (2010). Language ideologies–Evolving perspectives. Society and language use. 7 (3), 192-205.

Leary, M. R., & Tangney. J. P. (2012). Handbook of Self and Identity. The Guilford Press, New York London.

Leftwich, A., & Sen, K. (2010). 'Beyond Institutions: Institutions and Organizations in the Politics and Economics of Poverty Reduction— a Thematic Synthesis of Research Evidence,' IPPG Research Consortium on Improving Institutions for Pro-Poor Growth, University of Manchester

Leung, K., Bhagat, R.S., Buchan, N.R., Erez, M., & Gibson, C.B. (2005). Culture and international business: Recent advances and their implications for future research. *Journal of International Business Studies*, 36(4), pp. 357-378.

Lifegate newspaper. (2016). Tanzania, President Magufuli sets an example by picking up rubbish off the streets. Editorial staff, post for January 26. Accessed from: https://www.lifegate.com/tanzania-magufuli-cleans -up-streets

Little, M. (1991). Colonial Policy and Subsistence in Tanganyika 1925-1945, *The Geographical Review*, No 4.

Ludwig, K. (2017). From Plural to Institutional Agency: Collective Action II, Oxford: Oxford University Press.

Lustig, M.W., Koester, J., & Halualani, R. (2006). Intercultural competence: Interpersonal communication across cultures. Pearson /A and B.

Machangu, H. M. (2010). Elderly Women and Witchcraft Killings Among the Sukuma of Northern Tanzania: From the 1880s to the Present. *Afrika Zamani*, Nos 18 & 19, 2010 2011, pp. 181–198. Council for the Development of Social Science Research in Africa & Association of African Historians, 2013 (ISSN 0850-3079).

Maddox, G., Kimmbo, I. & Giblin, J. (Eds.). (1996). Custodian of the Land, Mkuki na Nyota.

Maddox K.B., & Gray S. A. (2002). Cognitive representations of African Americans: Re-exploring the role of skin tone. Personality and Social Psychological Bulletin. 28:250–259.

Maganda, F. F. (2008). The untold story: the agency of Sukuma educators in developing AIM mission schools in northwestern Tanzania, 1909-1970.

Maganda, D. (2014a). Gloswahilization of the African Mind: Language Ideology in Action. *Scholars Journal of Arts, Humanities and Social Sciences* (SJAHSS), 2 (4B), 550-558. Scholars Academic & Scientific Publishers (SAS), India.

Maganda, D. M., & Moshi, L.M. (2014). *The Swahili People and Their Language: A Teaching Handbook*. London, Adonis & Abbey Publishers.

Maganda, D. (2016). Why Don't You Understand? *Journal of Language and Literacy Education* (JoLLE), 12 (1). Georgia, USA.

Maganda, D. (2020). Learning that Brings Joy in an African Language Class: The Power of Reflection and Service Learning. In Esther Mukewa Lisanza & Leonard Muaka (Eds.). *African Languages and Literatures in the 21st Century*. Palgrave Macmillan.

Makeba, M. (Feb 2, 1960). Letter to the editor. What is in a name? Times. Accessed from: What's in a Name? | TIME.com

Makoye, K. (2013). Child marriage in Tanzania: cash for parents, problems for girls. Newspaper article, Thomson Reuters Foundation.

Malcom, D.W. (1953). Sukumaland an African People and their Country, London.

Marah, J. K. (2006), "The Virtues and Challenges in Traditional African Education." *The Journal of Pan African Studies,* 1(4): 15–24.

Masanja, P. (1992). Some Notes on the sungusungu movement, in P. Forster and S. Maghimbi (eds.), The Tanzanian Peasantry: economy in crisis, Aldershot: Avebury.

Masawe, B. (2019). Rice Production and its Impacts to Kwimba Society, SAUT.

Mazrui, A.A., & Mazrui, A.M. (1998). *The Power of Babel: Language and Governance in the African Experience*. London: James Currey Ltd.

McGregor, G. P. (2006). King's College Budo 1906-2006: A Centenary History. Fountain Publishers, Kampala, Uganda. ISBN 9970025449

McGrane, B. (1989). Beyond Anthropology: Society and the Other. New York, NY: Columbia University Press.

Mesaki, S. (1995). Witch-killing in Sukumaland,' in R. Abrahams (ed.), Witchcraft in Contemporary Tanzania, Cambridge: African Studies Centre.

Meek, B. (2007). "Respecting the Language of Elders: Ideological Shift and Linguistic Discontinuity in a Northern Athapascan Community." *Journal of Linguistic Anthropology*, 17 (1): 23–43. https://doi. org/10.1525/jlin.2007.17.1.23.

Meerterns, H. C. C., L. 0. Fresco & W. A. Stoop. (1996). Farming Systems Dynamics: Impact of Increasing Population Density and the Availability of Land Resources on Changes in Agricultural Systems. The Case of Sukumaland, Tanzania. Agriculture, Ecosystems, and Environment 56 (3), 203-215.

Miller, S. (2010). The Moral Foundations of Social Institutions: A Philosophical Study, New York: Cambridge University Press.

Mingari, F.M. (1983). Population and Production in Pre-colonial Ukara, MA Dissertation. University of Dar es Salaam.

Minkov, M., (2012). Cross-cultural analysis: The science and art of comparing the world's modern societies and their cultures. Sage Publications.

Mphande, L. (2006). "Naming and Linguistic Africanisms in African American Culture." Selected Proceedings of the 35th Annual Conference on African Linguistics, ed. John Mugane et al., 104-113. Somerville, MA: Cascadilla Proceedings Project.

Muendo, S. (2021). How Bongo stars embraced Magufuli and thrived. Standard Entertainment. Accessed from: https://www.standardmedia.co.ke/standard-entertainment/ article/2001406757/how-bongo-stars-embraced-magufuli-and-thrived

Mugarula, F. (2021). Tanzania: Magufuli Stresses Kiswahili Use. All Afrika. Accessed from https://allafrica.com/stories/202102030049.html

Mumbere, D. (2019). Tanzania's Magufuli offers Kiswahili books, teachers to Namibia. Africa News Accessed from: https://www.africanews.com/2019/05/29/tanzania-s-magufulioffers -kiswahili-books-teachers-to-namibia//

Mutethya, E. (2019). SADC adopts Kiswahili as 4th working language. China Daily. Accessed from https://www.chinadaily.com.cn/a/201908 /22/WS5d5ded0ba310cf3e35567377.html

Muscarella, O. W. (2008), "The Veracity of 'Scientific' Testing by Conservators' in E. Pernicka and S. von Berswordt-Wallrabe (eds.), Original – Copy – Fake? Examining the Authenticity of Ancient Works of Art – Focusing on African and Asian Bronzes and Terracottas. International Symposium Stiftung Situation Kunst/Ruhr-University Bochum, 17 and 18 February 2007. Mainz: Von Zabern, 9–18.

Muyingi, M. A. (2015). African Traditional Religion: A New Struggle for African Identity. *Journal of Theology*, 29 (1), p. 88-98.

Nagar, I. (2018). The Unfair Selection: A Study on Skin-Color Bias in Arranged Indian Marriages. Psychology, 8 (2), p. 1-8. https://doi.org/10.1177/2158244018773149

Ndunde, J. (Feb 3, 2021). Magufuli Promotes a Judge for Speaking Kiswahili. Business Today. Access from https://businesstoday.co.ke/magufuli-promotes-a-judge-for-speaking kiswahili/

Ndhlovu, F. (2008). Language and African development: Theoretical reflections on the place of languages in African Studies. *Nordic Journal of African Studies*, 17(2), 137–151.

Ngu˜gí wa Thiong'o (1986). Decolonizing the Mind: The Politics of Language in African Literature. Portsmouth, NH: Heinemann.

North, D. C. (1990). *Institutions, Institutional Change and Economic Performance*, New York: Cambridge University Press.

Nyerere, J. K. (1967b). Education for Self-reliance. Dar es Salaam: Government Printer.

Ochieng, W. & Maxon, R. (1992). An Economic History of Kenya, Nairobi: East African Educational Publishers Ltd.

Okita, S. I. (1992). African Culture in Search of Identity in A. Irele (ed.), African Education and Identity: Proceedings of the 5th Session of the International Congress of African Studies, Ibadan, December. London & New York: H. Zell Spectrum Books, 176–183.

Okpewho, I. (1992). African oral literature: Backgrounds, character, and continuity. Indiana University Press.

Owomoyela, O. (2002). Culture and customs of Zimbabwe. Greenwood Publishing Group.

relationships. Sex Roles: A Journal of Research. 56, 251–264.

Pambe, I. M. (1978). Symbols and Change in African Beliefs. Unpublished Doctoral Dissertation. Rome.

Peltzer, K., Pengpid, S., & James, C. (2016). The globalization of whitening: Prevalence of skin lighteners (or bleachers) use and its social correlates among university students in 26 countries. International Journal of Dermatology, 55, 165-172.

Penresa (2019), Visionary Leadership for a Prosperous and Progressive Tanzania. Accessed from: https://www.penresa.com/joseph-magufuli -visionary-leadership/

Pizam, A. (1993). Managing cross-cultural hospitality enterprises. The International Hospitality Industry: Organizational and Operational Issues, pp. 205-225.

Rattansi, A., & Phoenix, A. (2005). Rethinking youth identities: Modernist and postmodernist frameworks. Identity, 5, 97-123.

Reid, Marlene (1982). Patient/Healer Interactions in Sukuma Medicine. In Yoder, S. (ed.) African Health and Healing Systems: Proceedings of a Symposium. Los Angeles: Cross Roads Press.

Richmond, A., Myers, I., & Namuli, H. (2018). Urban Informality and Vulnerability: A Case Study in Kampala, Uganda. *Urban Science*, 2 (1), 22.

Robinson, J. L. (1992). African American body images: The roles of racial identity and physical attributes (Unpublished doctoral dissertation), Old Dominion University, Norfolk, VA Rockel, S. (1997). Caravan Porters of the Nyika: Labour, Culture and Society in 19th Tanzania, PhD Thesis, University of Toronto.

Rodger, J. (1954). Unyamwezi Development Report, Unpublished.

Rousseau, D. (1995). Psychological contracts in organizations: Understanding written and unwritten agreements. Sage publications.

Rubagumya, C. (2003). English medium primary schools in Tanzania: A new linguistic market in education? In Brock-Utne B, Desai Z, Qorro,

M; *Language of Instruction in Tanzania and South Africa*, Dar-es Salaam E&D Limited, 149-169.

Simmonds, F. N. (2005). Naming and identity, In Jarrett-Macauley, Delia. (Ed.), Reconstructing Womanhood, Reconstructing Feminism: Writings on Black Women. London and New York, Taylor & Francis e-Library.

Stephens DP, Few AL. (2007). The effects of images of African American women in Hip Hop on early adolescents' attitudes toward physical attractiveness and interpersonal

SABC News (2019). Accessed from: https://www.sabcnews.com/sabcnews/kiswahili-to-become-oneof-the -officiallanguagesin-sadc-bloc/

Salamn, R. (1992). Imaginary Homelands. New York: Granta.

Schein, E. H. (1992). Organizational culture and leadership. Jossey-Bass Publishers

Schein, E.H. (2010). Organizational culture and leadership. John Wiley & Sons.

Scott-Phillips, T. C. (2014). Speaking our Minds: Why Human Communication is Different and How Language Evolved to Make it Special. New York: Palgrave Macmillan.

Schieffelin, B. B., Woolard, K.A., & Kroskrity, P.V. (Eds). (1998). Language Ideologies: Practice and Theory. New York: Oxford University Press.

Senior, H.S. (1938). Sukuma Salt Caravans to Lake Eyasi, Tanganyika Notes and Records, N 6.

Shipman, T. (2007). Nerds Get Their Revenge as at Last It's Hip to Be Square. The Sunday Telegraph, 35.

Shin, A. (2015). "Locating King's College Budo: A study of Politics and Relationships in Colonial Buganda." A thesis submitted in partial fulfillment of the requirements for the degree of Bachelor of Arts in the Department of History, University of Michigan, USA, 1 April 2015.

Smith, P. B. (2011). Cross-cultural perspectives on identity: Conceptions and measurement. In S. J. Schwartz, K. Luyckx, & V. L. Vignoles (Eds.), Handbook of identity theory and research (pp. 249-266). New York, NY: Springer.

Speke, J.H. (1864). What led to the Discovery of the Source of the Nile, Blackwood Edinburgh and London.

Spencer-Oatey, H. (2004). Culturally speaking: Managing rapport through talk across cultures. A & C Black.

Spencer-Oatey, H., Franklin, P. (2012). What is culture? A compilation of quotations. Global Core Concepts, pp. 1-21.

Spreckels, J., & Kotthoff, H. (2009). Communicating Identity in Intercultural Communication, in Handbook of Intercultural Communication (eds), Helga Kotthoff and Helen Spencer Oatey (Berlin: Mouton de Gruyter, 2009), 415–19.

Sugimura, K. (2011). African Peasants and Moral Economy in Historical Perspective. In Maghimbi, S., N. I. Kimambo & K. Sugimura (eds.), Comparative Perspectives on Moral Economy: Africa and Southeast Asia. Dar esSalaam: Dares Salaam University Press, pp. 28-44.

Swilla, I. (2009). Languages of instruction in Tanzania: contradictions between ideology, policy, and implementation. *African Study Monographs*, 30 (1):1-14.

Tajfel, H., & Turner, J. (2004). The social identity theory of intergroup behavior. In J. Jost & J. Sidanius (Eds.), Political psychology: Key readings (pp. 276-293). New York: Psychology Press.

Taras, V., Rowney, J., & Steel, P. (2009). Half a century of measuring culture: Review of approaches, challenges, and limitations based on the analysis of 121 instruments for quantifying culture. *Journal of International Management*, 15(4), pp. 357-373.

Taylor, T. J. (1997). The Origin of Language: Why It Never Happened. *Language Sciences*, 19(1), 67–77.

Thomas, H. (1997). The Slave Trade: The Story of the Atlantic Slave Trade, 1440-1870. New York, NY: Simon & Schuster.

Trompenaars, F., & Hampden-Turner, C. (1997). Riding the waves of culture: Understanding cultural diversity in business. Nicholas Brealey.

Tonkin, H. (2003). Issues in Global Education: Language and Society. Occasional Papers from the American Forum for Global Education Number 178.

Ture, K., & Thelwell. E. M. (2003). Oriki: Ancestors and Roots. *The Massachusetts Review*, 44 (1/2), 97-111

Ullrich, R., Mittelbach, M., & Liebal, K. (2018). Scala Naturae: The Impact of Historical Values on Current "Evolution of Language" Discourse. *Journal of Language Evolution*, 3(1), 1–12.

Vats, R., & Thomas, S. A. (2015). Study on use of animals as traditional medicine by Sukuma Tribe of Busega District in North-western Tanzania. *Journal of Ethnobiology Ethnomedicine*, 11, 38. https://doi.org/10.1186/s13002-015-0001-y

Wade, T., & Bielitz, S. (2005). The differential effect of skin color on attractiveness, personality evaluations, and perceived life success of African Americans. Journal of Black Psychology, 31, 215-236.

Warner-Lewis, Maureen (2003). Central Africa in the Caribbean. Jamaica: UWI Press.

Wang, H. (2000). 'Informal institutions and foreign investment in China' Pacific Review, 13(4), pp. 525-556.

Watson, S., Thornton, C. G., & Engelland, B. T. (2010). Skin color shades in advertising to ethnic audiences: The case of African Americans. Journal of Marketing Communications, 16, 185-201.

Wells, S. (2002). The journey of man: a genetic odyssey. Princeton University Press, Digitised online, Google Books, ISBN 0-8129-7146-9.

White, D. (2020). 5 Reasons Why Obama Won the 2008 U.S. Presidential Election: Empathy and Genuine Help for Middle-Class Americans.

https://www.thoughtco.com/why-obama-won-2008-3325497.

Wiggins, S., & Davis, J. (2006). 'Economic Institutions,' IPPG Briefing Paper 3 at: http://www.ippg.org.uk/publications.htm

Wilhelms, R.W., Shaki, M.K., & Hsiao, C. F. (2009). How we communicate about cultures. Competitiveness Review: *International Business Journal*, 19 (2), pp. 96-105.

Woodson, C. G. (1990). The Miseducation of the Negro. Trenton, NJ: Africa World Press.

Woolard, K. A., & Schiefflein, B. B. (1994). Language ideology. *Annual Review of Anthropology*, 23, 55–82.

Woolman, D. C. (2001). "Educational Reconstruction and Post-colonial Curriculum Development: A Comparative Study of Four African Countries," *International Education Journal*, 2(5): 27–46.

Yep, G. A. (2002). "My Three Cultures: Navigating the Multicultural Identity Landscape," in Intercultural Communication: Experiences and Contexts, eds. Judith N. Martin, Lisa A. Flores, and Thomas K. Nakayama (Boston, MA: McGraw-Hill, 2002), 61.

Yule, G. (2006). *The study of language*. Cambridge University Press.

Zeleza, P.T. (2006). The inventions of African Identities and Languages: The Discursive and Developmental Implications. Selected Proceedings of the 36th Conference on African Linguistics, pp. 14–26. Somerville, MA: Cascadilla Proceedings Project.

ABOUT THE AUTHOR

DR. DAINESS MAGANDA is the Director of the African Languages Literatures and Cultures program in the Comparative Literature and Intercultural Studies Department (CLIS) at the University of Georgia. She teaches Swahili Language, Culture and Identity Linkages of the Swahili with the outside world, African Oral Literature, Introduction to African Languages and Culture, and How to Teach Less Commonly Taught Languages. Her publications focus on language, literacy, comparative education, intercultural studies, and identity issues. Her recent publication includes, *The Beauty of Diversity* (2021), and *Why do you ask me? From Dependency, to Self-Reliance, to Interdependency* (2021); *Negative Aspects of Bargaining as Identity Indicator of Africans in America* (2020).

CONNECT AND SHARE

If you enjoyed *Africa's Identity Revolution in the 21st Century*, please share this book with others and leave a review on Amazon.com or wherever books are sold. Connect with Dr. Dainess M. Maganda at www.imaduka.com.